# SELF-HYPNOSIS
## The key to success and happiness

### VALERIE AUSTIN

## Thorsons
*An Imprint of* HarperCollins*Publishers*

Thorsons
An Imprint of HarperCollins*Publishers*
77–85 Fulham Palace Road,
Hammersmith, London W6 8JB
1160 Battery Street,
San Francisco, California 94111-1213

Published by Thorsons 1994

10 9 8 7 6 5 4 3

A catalogue record for this book
is available from the British Library

ISBN 0 7225 2924 4

Printed and bound in Great Britain by
HarperCollinsManufacturing Glasgow

FOR MY SON

# CONTENTS

# ACKNOWLEDGEMENTS

To Peter, my love and thanks for years of patience. My agent and friend Roy Stockdill, whose encouragement, loyalty and occasional bullying helped me enormously.

Gil Boyne, who was responsible for introducing me to hypnosis in the first place.

Ormond McGill, an American gentleman in the true sense of the word, who brought dignity to his wonderful skill.

My colleagues and friends, Pat and Vic Leslie, for many years of comradeship.

Frank Lennon of the British National Register of Advanced Hypnotherapists.

Kay Kiernan for being a loyal friend in difficult times.

All my students, each one expanding my experience.

My thousands of patients.

Dr Michael a'Brook, for sending me many of the above and for his wonderful sense of humour.

Dr Acharyya for his faith and support.

Mavis, Azman and Nina, Hj Ayub Abdul Ghani, Malaysia Airlines, the Malaysian Tourist Board, and the lovely people of Langkawi for their help and guidance.

Uri Geller for his positiveness and for mending my watch.

Paul McKenna, a brilliant stage hypnotist.

And finally my fondness and admiration to Mr Adam, wherever you may be now.

# AUTHOR'S NOTE

You may find that the information in this book will help you, your relatives or your friends to relieve many problems, such as insomnia, smoking or weight control, to name but a few. But if you know someone who is in pain constantly and he or she would like some relief, the correct suggestions in the somnambulism state can give relief for hours. This is not a cure, just a natural relief, and should not be used to delay a visit to the doctor. But for someone with arthritic problems or pain-related illnesses or diseases, any relief will be a blessing.

# GLOSSARY OF TERMS

Words you will encounter throughout this book that sometimes cause confusion...

**Abreaction:** A raw emotion triggered off in hypnosis which then surfaces to the conscious level.

**Deepeners:** Specially selected words that form instructions for the purpose of guiding the mind into a much deeper feeling of relaxation in trance.

**Hypnosis:** Not sleep but a heightened state of awareness, similar to a day-dream. A state that a subject can be guided into by relaxation techniques or which can be induced by confusion or shock.

**Hypnotherapist:** A person who uses therapy while his or her subject is in hypnosis.

**Hypnotist:** A person who guides another into hypnosis.

**Induction:** A type of script carefully formed to guide the mind into relaxation.

**Suggestion:** Words that encourage the subconscious part of the mind into some sort of participation, either physically or mentally.

**Trance:** Many hypnotherapists do not like this word, but I am using it to establish a state of hypnosis. When a person is in a day-dream he or she is also in trance.

# one

# A VICTIM OF ONE'S MIND

I t all began with the car accident, the night I almost died—
the extraordinary twist of fate that led me to become a
hypnotherapist. I would never have believed at the time
that there would be a time in the future when I would count
the awful calamities and traumas I was to experience as
blessings, allowing me to put something back into life in
the form of helping people. If I had not had the car crash
I would not have had to seek treatment for a serious memory
loss and would never have been forced into discovering
hypnotherapy as a profession in the first place. The fact
that I did, albeit through a bizarre combination of circumstances, is why I am able to share my knowledge with you
now. Let me tell you about it...

The car was speeding through the pitch black night,
hurtling crazily out of control. I had no way of knowing
which direction it was taking. I was very frightened and
convinced I was going to die. Moments earlier I had been
travelling at high speed on the motorway when suddenly
I was forced to swerve violently to avoid a fleeing figure
running directly in front of me. It was 1.30 a.m. and there
was not even the palest glimmer of moonlight. Why on
earth was someone crossing the motorway on foot? Did
they intend to kill themselves? How ironic if that were so,

as that was precisely what I had been contemplating—a quick end to my life.

As I wrenched the steering wheel to avoid the ghostlike figure, the car skidded and lurched forward into the unknown, deep in the Staffordshire countryside. My headlights no longer picked out the friendly cats' eyes and I was spinning wildly towards thick undergrowth at the roadside.

I remembered being scared once before when I was a private pilot and wanted to qualify for a licence to fly at night. Unthinkingly I had chosen an extremely busy airport from which to do the two hours' necessary flying. I was suddenly queueing in line with jumbo jets and getting swirled around in their back-draught. But that experience paled in comparison to my terror now. At least then there had been landing lights, but here, in this horror, there was not even a moon to cast shadows. A jumble of confused thoughts and questions swirled in my mind as I was buffeted from side to side of the car like a limp rag doll. Each jolt sent a dull pain through my body. It was all happening in a few, fleeting moments yet it seemed like an eternity, as if I were watching myself in some ghastly, slow-motion video playback. Not long before I had actually been thinking about killing myself over a broken love affair. Now, in those terrifying moments as the car spun wildly out of control in the darkness, I knew I did not want to die. All I could think of was what would be the result once the car finally came to a halt. Would I be crippled or scarred for life? Would anybody find me so late at night, or would I have to die slowly, badly injured and alone? Had I been selfish? Was this my punishment? Would the nightmare ever end?

Then, as suddenly as it began, it was over. The car shuddered to a halt. Later I learned that it had hit three trees and plunged 30 feet down a ravine. Amazingly, however, I had not hit my head against the windscreen. I can remember sitting there dazed and shaking, yet still being able to think with remarkable clarity. The cassette player was still blasting out disco music, shattering the stillness of the night. Somehow, the windscreen wipers had got switched on during the crash. In my numbed and dazed state I could not remember how to switch them off. I was also alert enough to realize that there might have been a petrol leak and that the car might explode at any moment.

As I slowly and painfully eased myself out of the door, I felt as if I was the star of my very own horror film. The whole thing was so eerie and unreal. I was still trying to work out why my head had not hit the windscreen. I had not been wearing a seatbelt—this was the 1970s and there were still conflicting views about them—and the car had come to a dramatic stop. Later I learned that my head and face were the only parts of my body *not* to have been injured. It is something I have never been able to figure out to this day. Standing there, staring at my car, the shock of the accident must have distorted my thoughts. To me the car looked undamaged, yet actually it was a write-off. I had no clue as to where I was, I only knew I was somewhere off the M6. I was barefoot. My shoes must have come off in the car. My back felt strange. It was aching, but not too badly. I had heard of people walking after an accident even though they had been seriously injured. I wondered if it were possible to walk with a broken back. I seemed to be at the bottom of a deep hole, surrounded by trees and bushes. Somewhere above me I could hear the whine of the occasional car going by. I began to clamber up the steep embankment, forgetting my shoes in my desperate need to get help. Eventually I found myself on the hard shoulder, more through luck than judgement. I probably looked as if I had been attacked; I was completely dishevelled and distraught. A few cars passed and I prayed that I would not pass out on the hard shoulder and be run over by an unsuspecting driver pulling in for a rest. Then, my knight in shining armour came along at the wheel of a large lorry.

He helped me up into his cab. He said he had seen my headlights down off the roadside. He asked me if I had been drinking—I had not—and offered to take me home, even though I lived a hundred miles away in Blackpool. The pain was now so severe that just before I passed out I asked for an ambulance. I woke up in hospital, to be told by a doctor—to my amazement—that I had no bones broken and that he was discharging me. I was battered and bruised in every part of my body except my head but, apparently, hospital cutbacks meant that there was no bed available for me, even though it was now around 3.30 a.m. The policemen who had been called out to the accident called me Cinderella because they found my shoes in the car. No one knew quite what to do with me, but the nurses felt sorry for me and gave me a bed in a corridor until the morning.

Shock does strange things to the system. The thoughts I had had earlier during that fateful drive—the overwork, the broken romance and other traumas that had led me briefly to contemplate suicide—flitted across my mind but only made me feel glad to be alive. They did not seem so important now. Maybe, I pondered, this accident was an escape of sorts after all. Next morning, still in excruciating pain, I took a train back to Blackpool. The friend who picked me up at the station was shocked by my appearance. I was a sorry sight—hunched over, with bedraggled hair, crumpled clothes and a tear-streaked face. It took me a year to recover, enduring six months of severe pain as my spine slowly healed. I regained my health but my income had gone. Previously I had earned a good living as a top sales representative and had also run my own promotional company. But because I still could not bend sufficiently to ease my way into a car, I was unfit to drive. I had to find other ways to earn a living, so I enrolled in a secretarial course to learn typing, shorthand and advanced French. It was only then that I began to realize that the damage I had suffered in the accident was more sinister than I had imagined and was not confined just to physical problems.

At first I thought I was just being slow at picking things up, though that was unusual for me as I had always been a fast learner. I was already a touch typist but I could not even do that properly without making dozens of mistakes. I found I was not able to understand even the simplest things. Worse still, my friends began to notice that the day after an evening out I would have no memory of the night before—nothing to do with alcohol, either. I could not recall people or places. To my enormous embarrassment I was having to ask lifelong friends who they were. I became what others considered 'eccentric', constantly losing things, never ready for a date or appointment on time. I also began to dress oddly. When I confided my symptoms and worries to my doctor he told me my head had been shaken up so much in the accident that it would take some time to 'settle'. He remarked that I had touched the Pearly Gates and was very lucky still to be alive.

Another 12 months went by and my memory had not improved one jot, so I went back to my doctor. He suggested the problem was probably trauma-based. He suggested I find a doctor who was also a hypnotherapist, but warned me that it would not be easy to find a good one. No one knew the nightmare I was going through because outwardly I looked fine. But I could not perform even the simplest tasks, such as filing. I was a totally disruptive influence to those I worked with. I would start a job and move on to something else, forgetting to finish the first task. I had begun to drive again but I would lose my car keys, go to look for them in my handbag and then forget, when I had found my handbag, what I had wanted it for. I would even forget that I was supposed to be going out at all. I would spend hours looking for things, totally absorbed in the search and unaware of the passage of time. I lost all my money. I could not keep a job because I was unemployable. I tried writing down a list of things to do each day but it was useless—I would simply forget I had made a list!

I suffered two-and-a-half years of this mental fog, during which I got little help or sympathy from anyone except close friends. My father refused even to believe it, thinking I was just being flippant. It was only when my mother suffered a fall and was taken unconscious to hospital that he realized how serious my condition was—because I *forgot* all about my mother's accident and went to a party rather than visit her in hospital. My son would be left outside my house on weekend breaks from boarding school while I was off staying with friends, having forgotten I even had a son. My life was a trail of confusion. I will give you an another example of just how bad my impairment was: I took a temporary job as an assistant to a film director. During my brief employment I was given a short memo to be typed and distributed to a dozen people in the film unit, with all their names listed at the top. I spent most of a morning typing and retyping it, trying really hard to get it right. Finally satisfied, I made a dozen copies and distributed them to the relevant people. It was not long before it was brought to my attention that I had left out one thing—the memo itself! I had been so preoccupied with getting the list of names right, I had forgotten about the message!

Very embarrassing.

Indirectly, though, this job was my entrée into the film world. I went to California, initially in search of a cure for my amnesia. I had read a story about a 'wonder' drug that was apparently only available in the US. I never found it, but I did find a husband. I fell in love with an American producer and writer and we became engaged. When I returned to Britain, he phoned me every single night just to make sure I still remembered him! This was a bit comical, but actually it also gave me an idea. I was still praying for a cure for my memory loss and badly in need of some money to pay for it, so I sold my story to a newspaper in the hope that someone would see it and be tempted to offer help. The story appeared in papers in both Britain and America— one of them splashed it with the headline: 'Will Bride Remember Her Husband?'

My ploy worked. A famous American hypnotist called

Gil Boyne, a stage hypnotist turned hypnotherapist who has treated many Hollywood stars, happened to be lecturing in the UK and read my story. Boyne tracked me down and said that when I returned to the US he would treat me free if he could use me as a 'guinea pig' in front of his students at his training school in Los Angeles.

Boyne was as good as his word. He did precisely what he had promised and cured me of my memory loss before his entire class. To me it seemed the session only lasted a few minutes but later I discovered I was in hypnosis for an hour and a half. One session and I was cured! That was the day before I was due to be married. After a terrible two-and-a-half period of not being able to remember anything, I was now ready to start a new life in the US, with a new husband and a memory that worked!

Ironically, though, my cure did cause a strain in my marriage, almost from the start. The new me was quite a shock for my American husband, who knew me only as a wacky eccentric who was totally dependent on him. He had never met the 'real' me, an independent, responsible and quite astute businesswoman.

Gil Boyne recognized the important contacts I had made through my husband, who was a senior editor on one of the top show business newspapers in the US. Boyne was aware of the publicity potential in my cure. He hired me to do promotional work for him and I became his 'pet amnesia victim', accompanying him on various television and radio shows. At the time I still had no real serious interest in hypnosis. I was too busy enjoying myself, travelling, building up a good business, interviewing the rich and famous and editing a column in my husband's newspaper.

For two years everything went swimmingly. Then...disaster struck again. On one of my frequent return visits back home to Britain a string of family deaths, accidents and traumas so devastated me that I suffered a relapse into amnesia. Incredibly, the newspaper headline came true and I actually forgot that I had a husband in the US! I never went back to him.

I spent the next four years in another mental fog. My confusion and eccentric behaviour were, if anything, even worse than they had been before. I had a memory retention span of no more than 24 hours at the most, so planning ahead was impossible. I had to live literally for each day alone. One of the things I noticed was how cruel people could be, though mostly unintentionally. I lost count of how many folk joked to me that they would not mind having a memory loss, too!

Throughout the whole sorry saga, I tried work as a journalist, a pop group agent, selling industrial diamonds, selling films and TV pop shows and, holding an Equity card, acting as an extra. Many times I forgot to pick up my salary.

I launched a magazine (it only lasted three issues), while at the same time working in a pub. The customers quickly got used to being charged the wrong money. The magazine failed, mainly due to my inefficiency. I was constantly losing copy and generally causing havoc.

Then I came upon a British hypnotherapist who was an associate of Gil Boyne's. This man was conducting a training school and was well versed in American hypnotherapy methods. I asked him to help. He did and I regained my memory once more. But this time I took a deeper interest in the whole subject.

I watched the students training and for the first time the thought came into my mind that I might enter the profession myself. My motives initially were selfish. I thought that if I understood more about the whole thing I might at least be able to help myself retain my memory, or be able to call upon professional colleagues who could assist me. The more I learned about hypnotherapy, however, the more I came to see its tremendous value and its potential for helping people.

So that is how I became a hypnotherapist. I trained in Britain and later in the US where, because of my 'celebrity' status as Gil Boyne's star 'guinea pig', I was lucky enough to receive some rather special treatment. However, there was a price to pay as well—as they say, there is no such thing as a free lunch! I found to my dismay that video tapes of me being treated in front of Boyne's class were circulating in the hypnotherapy world for other therapists and their students to see. There were all my most private secrets publicly laid bare on tape and recorded for posterity. Many thousands of clients later, however, I have never regretted embarking on my new life and new career. I went through so many different traumas brought on by my memory loss that I found it easy to sympathize with my clients. I seemed to have had all of their problems myself at one time or another.

With everything I have learned since then, I now know that when I had my memory loss the car accident was only the catalyst. The problems actually stemmed from eight years before, from an even earlier trauma when I had witnessed a terrible crime. New hypnotherapy techniques cut through the more superficial problems of life and go straight to the heart of the real trauma. But it takes a special kind of training to find them and, unfortunately, few therapists are taught these techniques.

## A BRIEF LOOK AT HYPNOSIS IN THE PAST TWO CENTURIES

Before we come to the main purpose of this book, it may help your understanding of hypnosis to know just a little of its history and background. Important dates include:

- **1775:** Franz Mesmer developed healing by 'animal magnetism', which was later renamed hypnosis.
- **1784:** Count Maxime de Puysegut discovered a form of deep trance he called somnambulism.
- **1821:** First reports of painless surgery in France using magnetism.
- **1841:** A Scottish doctor, James Braid, changed the name from magnetism to hypnosis. He established it as a psychological phenomenon.
- **1845–53:** A surgeon, James Esdaile, performed 2,000 operations—even amputations—with the patients under hypno-anaesthesia and feeling no pain.
- **1883–1887:** Sigmund Freud became interested in hypnosis and began to practise it.
- **1894:** Freud abandoned hypnosis to concentrate on developing psychoanalysis.
- **1947:** Hypnosis was being used by dentists in the US.
- **1950:** Societies and associations for hypnosis started to sprout up.

- **1958:** The American Medical Association approved the therapeutic use of hypnosis by physicians.

In short, it took nearly two centuries for hypnosis to be recognized as a therapy by the medical associations; after another 30 years-plus it still has not been fully accepted by the medical profession or the public in general.

It is true that there have been many casualties of hypnosis. However, these were not the clients but the practitioners, the brilliant men and women throughout history who have succeeded in hypnotherapy but who failed miserably in marketing the controversial phenomenon of hypnosis. Clouded in mystery, the dangers of the trance state have been propagated by the ignorant. Every time hypnosis obtains a foothold as a form of cure, those using it, whether medical professionals or lay people, are exposed to ridicule.

The vulnerability of hypnosis is that it does not have a 100 per cent success rate, therefore it is very easy to claim to disprove it scientifically. In Western society we demand proof for everything. Homoeopathy cannot be 'proved'. The fact that it works does not seem to interest the sceptics, however, who demand proof according to their rules. Since you cannot prove the existence of the subconscious—let alone what its function is—according to some people's criteria of proof, hypnotherapy is nothing less than quackery. However, we must bear in mind that science itself is not infallible. At one time it was 'scientifically proven' that the bumble bee could not fly—and, indeed, that the earth was flat.

Because of the lack of finance for research, hypnosis is still fighting to gain the recognition it deserves. Only as recently as mid-1992 has there been acceptable scientific proof that hypnosis does work, published in the *New Scientist* (June 1993). Having undertaken one of the largest surveys ever recorded of stopping smoking methods, spanning several continents, the *New Scientist* came out with the verdict: 'Hypnosis is proven to work.' Indeed, hypnosis was found to be streets ahead of anything else on the market when it came to helping people to stop smoking. Hypnosis is as natural as time itself and a gift to us all, once we know of its existence.

Although hypnosis has been practised, albeit under different names virtually since the beginning of human existence, it came to the attention of Western civilization with Maximilian Hell, a monk who introduced it to Franz Mesmer, the Austrian physician, in the 1700s. Mesmer treated patients with what he regarded as an 'animal magnetism' that pervaded the whole universe. His name and methods passed into everyday usage in the words mesmerize and mesmerism. Many years later, James Braid renamed this magnetism hypnosis, after the Greek word for sleep. This was actually a very unfortunate choice which has caused major misunderstandings of hypnotism ever since. For, although the hypnotized are *not* asleep, they give the impression that they are, which is very misleading.

The history of hypnosis is as chequered as that of some of its practitioners, and trying to outlaw it is as difficult as trying to stop video piracy. Some hypnotists have not exactly been the best advertisements themselves for the profession. When therapists put enough energy into promoting themselves and then revel in the publicity gained from evaluations of their supposedly 'miraculous' treatments, the result usually is that they find their egos expanding out of all proportion to their skills. Success can be its own worst enemy! Forgotten is the main rule: that they are only the experts guiding their clients to make the change. It is the clients who actually make the change in themselves, not the therapist.

Real hypnosis has many celebrated professionals. Of the many fascinating workshops I attended in the US, the one that most took my attention for its historical grounding was a session at which the speaker was Morgan Eaglebear, great-great grandson of the legendary Native American chief, Geronimo. Eaglebear is a practising hypnotherapist and healer. He explained how this form of natural healing had been used for generations among Native American tribes. They did not call it hypnosis but it was the same thing. A young tribal member would be chosen to learn the history of the tribe, which was never written down but just passed on by word of mouth. To ensure that the history was sound and the memory of the initiate was not impaired, the chosen one had to go through tests of bravery to prove his fitness. He was then strung up by his skin, while in a trance state. In this trance form, he felt no pain and each elder of the tribe would visit him and relay a part of the history. This went on for many days.

One test to tell if you are in a deep form of hypnosis is to check for anaesthesia. If you feel no pain, then you are in a deep trance. I suppose these Native Americans were unwilling, given that the passing on of tribal knowledge was so important, to take the chance that the chosen initiate was merely feigning a trancelike state. By hanging him up by his skin they could be sure he was definitely in a deep hypnotic trance. The famous film that depicts this particular practice, *A Man Called Horse* (1969), starred Richard Harris and showed this test of bravery using the most sophisticated cinema effects of the day. Of course, there was no mention of the trance state in the film.

To get back to the workshop, there in front of me was Eaglebear, this marvellously built and very charismatic man who wore his hair long and dressed as a brave, a living embodiment of Native American history. He lifted his shirt to show me the scars proving he had undergone the great test of bravery. I spoke to him after the lecture and he told me that the old Native American tribes used hypnosis on the newborn. Facing the danger of the campsite being attacked in the middle of the night, the tribal members had to ensure that no baby would cry and give the campsite's location away. Mothers would therefore train their babies to go into a trance, talking soothingly to them and gently brushing the flat of their hands past their babies' eyes, gently closing them. This was a practice that was passed from generation to generation. Whenever the mother's hand passed over her child's eyes in this fashion, the child would become silent. He also explained that the women, when giving birth, did not know it was supposed to be painful and so, not expecting pain, did not experience any. It seemed to me that there was so much that we of the so-called technologically advanced societies could learn from these ancient wisdoms.

# WHAT WILL HYPNOSIS DO FOR YOU?

Let us now turn to the real purpose of this book—showing you how you can use hypnosis to improve your own life or to help others to solve their problems. This book is written to present the power that you possess to change your attitudes, which in turn changes your behaviour so that you can achieve exactly what you want. You can choose your own personality and begin to programme it into your mind. Your mind will follow the instructions you give it—as long as these instructions do not go against your interests for survival.

Hypnosis is the gateway to reprogramming an old or unwanted behaviour pattern or creating a new, positive one. It allows you to accept certain thoughts, which in turn change your attitude, so that you can do the things you want to do—or not do the things you do not want to do but cannot seem to stop doing. You may want to stop smoking, lose weight, or treat a phobia—for example fear of success, snakes or spiders. You may want to increase your productivity, improve your love life, bring back the love into your marriage, speed read, fly a plane, be more confident and outgoing or enable yourself, with full concentration, to pass exams or a driving test. Whatever you'd like to achieve hypnosis can help.

# WHAT IS HYPNOSIS?

Everyone can be hypnotized. In fact, everyone goes into hypnosis every day of their lives. Every time you day-dream you are in a form of hypnosis. You can put yourself in hypnosis now. Just close your eyes and imagine yourself the last time you were eating a meal in a restaurant or in someone's home. See what details you can bring forward. The decor of the room in which you were eating, whom you were with, what kind of atmosphere was present. See if you can remember the conversation—then open your eyes. What you experienced was a very light form of hypnosis. If you were to be put into a deeper state your vision would be more focused and accurate, for the more you practise hypnosis the more you develop your imagination.

### Are You Visual?

To check whether you are a visual person or not (for the purpose of hypnosis) you can do a simple test. Close your eyes and think of a chair—any chair. When you have it in your thoughts, 'see' what colour it is, then open your eyes. Ask yourself if you actually 'saw' the chair in your imagination or just 'knew' what it looked like. There is a difference, if you think about it. If you saw it, then you are considered a visual person.

Freud's research showed that two-thirds of the population were visual. I decided to make my own study on well over a thousand clients and the results more or less substantiated this figure. This was important to me because I am one of the non-visual people, that small segment of the population who have trouble visualizing. We can imagine what it is like to be visual, but it is impossible for a visual person to understand how someone can imagine without actually seeing. If you have a hypnotherapist who is visual and you are not, there will definitely be communication problems. This distinction has in the past caused a multitude of problems. It has resulted in there being many inexperienced hypnotherapists who have believed their clients awkward and 'hard to hypnotize'. This is how the myth grew that not everyone can be hypnotized. A proficient hypnotherapist knows that everyone can be hypnotized. Of course degrees of susceptibility vary, but it only takes less susceptible people a little longer to be able to build their belief structure.

The simple 'visual/non-visual' test above solves the problem. Try it out on your friends as practice. If someone says he cannot 'see' the chair but just knows what it looks like, explain that this is not unusual. A third of the population does not visualize. For these people a hypnotherapist must abandon the words 'visualize' or 'see' which might otherwise be used, and instead use the word 'imagine'—in the way you did with the chair. I was told by three hypnotherapists I was difficult to hypnotize. This could not have been further from the truth.

## Hypnosis Is Not Sleep!

Hypnosis is a heightened state of awareness. While in hypnosis you are aware of everything that is happening around you. Conversations, the telephone ringing, any noise that occurs. It is the same as if you were day-dreaming. When you are guided into a relaxed state your imagination is more focused because your conscious is occupied. In order to protect your 'occupied consciousness' another facility, which we call the subconscious, comes forward. If anything untoward happens, the subconscious immediately alerts your conscious and you terminate the day-dream.

Imagine you are driving along a motorway and you start day-dreaming about what you will be doing when you arrive at your destination. If you get sufficiently involved in this day-dream you go into a sort of auto-pilot to drive your car. You know there is traffic about but you are not fully conscious of it. Then, after a few miles, you suddenly come out of the day-dream and realize you have not noticed the scenery and the traffic. You probably think to yourself that you might well have had an accident if you had continued in this state. The truth of the matter is that if the car in front of you had put its brake lights on suddenly, your subconscious mind would have come forward during your day-dream to protect you. It would bring your conscious back in a split second to deal with the emergency. As soon as your conscious mind becomes occupied, your subconscious always come forward to protect you. All your senses link up with it and even become more aware at that level. Say there was a smell of rubber in the car. Your subconscious would alert your conscious and bring you out of the day-dream to attend to it. Or if there was an unfamiliar sound in the engine, the same instant awareness would come into operation.

Another example: allow yourself to imagine you are on a tube or train. You have quite a long way to go, so you are day-dreaming. In fact, you are oblivious to what is going on around you. If suddenly there was an odd sound alongside you, you would immediately become aware of it and respond accordingly. Therefore, if the sound was threatening, within a split second your conscious would be fully alert and ready to 'fight or flee.' That is the term psychologists use to describe our pre-historic instinct for survival. If the sound is not threatening, then you would just carry on in your day-dream trance state. You are always protected, even though you may not have been aware of such sophisticated processes going on in your mind.

This, then, is the difference between hypnosis and sleep. When you are asleep you are not protected in this way. But your subconscious is using this very valuable time for 'internal affairs', sorting out the new information to be filed away, etc. When you are anaesthetized or have certain drugs, your memory can bring forward incidents that have occurred while you were in this state. Medical staff in hospitals are careful what they say during operations, due to fairly recent findings proving that patients have subconsciously heard what has been said when anaesthetized and have later suffered irrational behaviour as a direct result.

A hypnotherapist is a person who uses therapy while his or her client is in the relaxed state of hypnosis. Good hypnosis is important to good therapy. The reason hypnosis is used in therapy is to relax the mind; in so doing the subconscious comes forward. When your conscious is relaxed, new information has more chance of being accepted, which is why at this point the subconscious can be accessed and behaviour reprogrammed. You are aware of what is going on the whole time and you are being guided by the therapist, not unlike a computer expert showing you how to work a computer.

In hypnosis you cannot be made to do anything you do not want to do! You have a failsafe survival trigger mechanism that protects you at all times.

## WHO IS SUSCEPTIBLE TO HYPNOSIS?

This question conjures up an amazing and controversial set of opinions, based on various people's belief structures. I can tell you what I understand, in the knowledge that my reasoning will probably be severely attacked by some. Nevertheless, my opinions are based on my experiences in working with well over 2,000 clients.

Everyone is susceptible to hypnosis to differing degrees. If, however you want to break the question down and ask who is susceptible to going into hypnosis immediately, then the answer is completely different. About a third of a group of people at any one time are likely to be susceptible to being put instantly into hypnosis. That is why the stage hypnotist can feel secure that there will always be a good percentage of his audience he will be able to work with, ensuring a fast-moving show. A brief explanation of the nature of stage hypnosis may help you to understand a little more.

First, the hypnotist will do a quick suggestibility test to decide whom he is going to use in his act. Normally he chooses a simple task, such as instructing the audience to clasp their hands together. He suggests that their hands will literally stick together as if super-glued and that, whatever they do, they will not be able to unclasp them. The hypnotist uses confusing and repetitive instructions, then he asks the members of the audience to try and unclasp their hands. Those who do unclasp their hands are not used in the act. Of the members of the audience who still have their hands clasped together, he will ascertain whether they are pretending or whether they really are in hypnosis. His experience weeds

out the odd cheat. Those few who are left are considered
to be in hypnosis and, therefore, susceptible.

Susceptibility in hypnosis has nothing to do with intelligence or trying too hard either way. The more someone is
hypnotized, the more susceptible he or she becomes. Very
susceptible people in hypnosis will still refrain from doing
something that they find unacceptable. The grey area is
that in hypnosis people may not have as many inhibitions
as they would normally and may, therefore, be more daring.

## WHY HYPNOSIS IS SO EASY TO LEARN

(Only fools laugh at what they do not understand!) To
learn hypnosis takes only a few minutes. To understand
why and how it works will take rather longer. If the basics
are taught correctly, the learning is quick and easy because
everything about the subject is fascinating. It is far simpler
to learn than operating a computer. If you have any
experience of computers, you will remember how difficult
the manuals were to understand at first. That was not
because the computer itself was difficult but because the
manual's explanations were at fault. A good basic training
in any subject saves you hours of unnecessary hard work.
Take away the unnecessarily difficult words that confuse
the brain, interfering with retention and concentration,
replace them with simple instructions, and you have a quick
and easy new skill at your fingertips.

Hypnosis is a very easy subject to understand. Anyone
with normal intelligence can be taught how to hypnotize
or be hypnotized. Of course some hypnotherapy courses

can be padded out to two years in length if they include study of psychology and the history of the subject, including its early masters such as Freud and Jung. Although this added information is quite fascinating it can end up being a bit too much, reminiscent of the old saying about 'not being able to see the wood for the trees'.

Hypnotherapy can be split up into two basic categories: suggestion therapy, which is what is being taught in this book, and what I shall call advanced hypnotherapy, which is actually accessing the subconscious in therapy and communicating with it.

The techniques and methods can be taught in one to three weeks, depending on the degree of advancement. Any other length of time would only be necessary to show different techniques to come to the same conclusion. I have found that a 50-hour practical course is sufficient. If you want a comparison, this about the same amount of time necessary to qualify for a private pilot's licence.

## Is Hypnosis Dangerous?

This is the most common belief of all—and the greatest fallacy.

You cannot be hypnotized against your will! You have to agree to it. But you can be caught off-guard. If any unacceptable suggestions were then made, you would nevertheless have the choice of either terminating the voluntary trance state or continuing with it. You can be persuaded or told to do something but you still are able to reason and you can still say 'No.' You are, after all, still awake, as mentioned earlier.

Unfortunately many books on the subject, and even some courses, may lead us to believe that hypnosis is not only complicated but dangerous. If this were true there would surely have been some legislation by now to weed out the unsavoury charactors who were abusing this most natural healing gift. The fact is, the only danger is that, if done incorrectly, hypnosis just will not work.

Many people have been mislead into thinking of hypnosis as 'brainwashing'. The simple fact is that people who are being hypnotized just will not accept a suggestion in hypnosis that is damaging to them. In order to be brainwashed you need three vital ingredients: pain, drugs and hypnosis. Those who say they were made to do something by a hypnotist or hypnotherapist against their will, then they should eliminate the word 'made' and replace it with 'conned'— and you do not need to be hypnotized to be conned. *You always have a choice as to whether you are going to do what the hypnotist says or not.*

Do not be persuaded into thinking hypnosis is dangerous, because it is not. A lot of the misapprehensions about hypnosis stem from ignorance, while some of them, it must be said, are spread by practitioners of hypnotism themselves. They fear that too many people will realize how natural a healing process hypnosis is, thereby taking away their importance as 'miracle workers'—whether on stage or in healing. Although the hypnotist is well aware that it is the person in hypnosis who is accomplishing any act or change, unfortunately the hypnotist's ego sometimes intervenes and halts the otherwise natural progress by shrouding in mystery the most natural self-healing gift known to humanity.

# two

# THE SUBCONSCIOUS

In order to have a good, working understanding of hypnosis it is helpful to have an insight into how the mind works in general. This can be explained very simply. You do not need to know about the elaborate, sophisticated workings of the mind; a basic explanation will be sufficient.

The mind is made up of two parts: the subconscious and the conscious. The subconscious part of the mind functions automatically. It is not the thinking part, it is the doer. Before the age of approximately five years old, our ability to learn is at its peak. All the information passed on to us from our parents, teachers, etc. goes directly to the subconscious, which files it away immediately. This is why if you tell a toddler that a wall is black when it is white the child will just accept this, where an older child would challenge you. As the child progresses another facility comes into operation: the conscious.

The conscious part of the mind acts like an editor of a newspaper, who chooses which stories will be carried in each edition, which will be filed away to use another day, and which can be discarded. There is only a certain amount of knowledge that can be held at any one time in the forefront of the mind to which the conscious has immediate access. When this forefront is fully occupied, any additional information coming through is stored away in the mind's 'filing system'. Just like the busy editor who has an assistant in charge of the filing, the conscious passes over control of the sophisticated filing system to the subconscious. And just as when the editor's assistant is absent the editor may have problems finding a file, the conscious has no idea how to work the unfamiliar, complicated controls of the subconscious filing system.

Everything we have ever done, said, heard, smelled or seen is stored away, in fact. In hypnosis the subconscious can be easily accessed and the memories of an incident retrieved and looked at in detail. The police find this particularly useful in uncovering information—such as the record of a number-plate or the description of the face of an attacker—when victims' or witnesses' immediate, conscious memory has been erased by shock.

In my practice in Harley Street I often take clients back in regression (a term used to describe taking someone back in hypnosis to an earlier memory) to the time when they first walked as a child. They can see what they wore (sometimes just a nappy), what their parents were like and how they looked, even to describing their hairstyles and what they were saying. This shows how fantastic a system the brain is and how easy it is to retrieve information.

There are many obstacles preventing certain information being directly available to the conscious mind. Accessing the subconscious overcomes these obstacles immediately. Remember, the subconscious is the automatic part of the mind and will take orders. If you ask for a certain memory to be brought forward, it retrieves the required information as instructed. If the memory is attached to a trauma, the whole package comes forward.

By accessing data straight from the subconscious the information is not edited and, consequently, you may touch on a particularly distressing incident. This unhappy memory may cause the person in hypnosis to undergo what is called an *abreaction*. This means that he or she is *in the middle of* the emotion and may burst into tears. This outburst can sometimes be very exaggerated, due to the trance and the lifting of inhibitions. To the untrained it can be quite frightening and is another reason why hypnosis has for so long been rumoured to cause people actual mental or psychological harm.

This concentrated raw emotion will usually only come to the surface while a person is being treated with advanced hypnosis, but there are occasions, though very rare, when it can surface during suggestion hypnosis—just as you can strike a raw nerve, by accident, in the middle of an innocent conversation.

I became aware that abreactions are in fact not that serious and that anyone can have one without warning. Just watching a film, listening to the radio or hearing someone speak can trigger off an emotional memory. When I had my memory loss I was told that someone whom I knew had died. I took it in but did not react. Six weeks later I was walking through the busy passageways at a London tube station when I suddenly burst into tears. Something had triggered off the memory of my friend's death.

The conscious is the thinking, logical part of the mind. If there is no reasonable explanation for a behaviour pattern the conscious will invent one that seems to it to be logical. You can see an example of this thought process in the typical smoker. Asked why he smokes his reply could be simply: 'I enjoy it.' Yet this same person will probably have a list of objections to smoking as well, such as 'I hate the smell,' etc. He may even claim that he wants desperately to quit. There is definitely a conflict here, but not one so great or complex that the smoker cannot easily be treated by hypnosis. Because smoking is rarely trauma-related, quitting with the help of hypnosis is a straightforward matter.

The person who overeats may say he does so because he enjoys it. This may be partly true but there are most likely other, deeper motivations. He may crave comfort, protection or even punishment, and overeating satisfies this craving. We all have to eat to live and therefore we are all programmed to be tempted by food. Our senses are tuned to pick up on the smell, taste, texture and look of food. Our bodies are also programmed to provide a feeling of fullness or satisfaction when we have eaten enough. When there is some trauma-based condition, however, a new behaviour pattern is created causing a person to overeat not just because he enjoys it, but for other reasons as well.

The answer from the conscious of 'Because I enjoy it' for the two entirely different problems of smoking and overeating gives little indication of what treatment is necessary. In either case the answer is the most 'logical' the conscious could generate, given its limited information. The full story is filed away in the subconscious filing system and, if trauma-based, is probably completely unknown to the conscious.

When I had my memory problem I was regularly told that I should write a list of things I needed to do each day. If you know you have a list to look up, then this method works. But if as in my case you forget you have even written a list in the first place, then this 'solution' is useless. Because I was not aware I had written a list it would be treated as just another scrap of paper. I did not associate it with a list of things to do and, therefore, either threw it away or popped it into a drawer for inspection at another time.

If the conscious has no knowledge of the information that has slipped unnoticed into the subconscious, it has no cause to retrieve it. The subconscious receives no instruction from the conscious to look for the stored, relevant information, so it is not supplied. Hypnosis allows us access to the subconscious so the files can be retrieved and the underlying causes of a problem can be looked at. Therefore, it is not surprising that what the conscious mind thinks is the logical reason for a habit or problem bears little resemblance to its actual cause.

There are differing beliefs about how the subconscious works. Some think it has an intelligence equal to that of a bright six year old. I prefer to believe it is completely automatic—like a sophisticated computer system that can hold a conversation and talk as if it were human only because it has been programmed that way.

## WHY IS A BAD HABIT SO HARD TO BREAK?

The subconscious is often called 'the unconscious' in many teachings. I prefer 'subconscious' because this term is not so misleading. The word 'unconscious' perpetuates the popular myth that hypnosis is sleep. This brings us to the importance of another misunderstood facet of human behaviour, the bad habit. People are surprised that bad habits are hard to break but rarely consider what a blessing it is to be able to keep good ones. Imagine learning to ice-skate or drive a car and then suddenly losing the habit! The consequences could be fatal.

To form a habit you practise it and, when practised enough, it becomes automatic. You first consciously work at it, then, if you continue for a long enough period, the subconscious takes over. The subconscious does not judge whether it is a good or bad habit. It presumes that if you do it enough, then you must want it to be permanent. Likewise, when you want to put an end to a habit you have to practise until you 'automatically' stop doing it.

The subconscious is programmed to ensure that the conscious retains this newly-learned habit. Part of the 'job' of the subconscious is to create an obstacle course to prevent any change to the acquired habit.

Once the subconscious has taken a habit on board it provides an 'urge'. It is, therefore, the subconscious that we need to access in order to persuade it to cancel the programme that triggers this 'urge'. Hypnosis provides instant access to the subconscious and allows an immediate change of attitude which, in turn, changes the unwanted behaviour. Simply put, with hypnosis it is not necessary to practise unlearning a habit because the work has already been completed. The conscious mind is more or less bypassed— only, however, if it is in the individual's interest.

If you were to decide at a later date that you wanted to regain an old habit, very little practice would be needed. The programme would already be set and could easily be retrieved. For example, if you had not ridden a bike for 10 years and then had a go, you might be a bit shaky at first but, nevertheless, your confidence would soon return. Or, just walking down a flight of stairs, try thinking which foot goes where and notice how difficult it is. Since you have formed the habit it has become an automatic instinct and you are no longer conscious of the action. Consider amnesia victims: whatever else they may have forgotten, they always remember how to open doors, how to talk and how to perform most habitual, simple tasks. I should know, if anyone does!

Just as you can eliminate a bad habit without practice through hypnosis, it is also feasible that you can create a good one in the same way. I have proved this in developing a speed reading programme in which I can guarantee at least to double a person's reading speed, while increasing retention and concentration, in less than three hours (20 minutes if there is no trauma involved which may be preventing the subject from accepting the speed reading technique). To speed read properly you have to use a pointer, such as a pen, pencil or even your finger, to lead your eyes across the page. Without hypnosis it could take as long as 40 hours' practice to master this. It may sound simple but involves a complicated procedure, linking eye movement and the correct maximum speed for optimum concentration. To achieve the 100 per cent success rate I have been able to claim with my speed reading clients there may be a need for advanced methods of hypnosis, but suggestion-only therapy can reach a healthy 60 per cent of those who try it. Obstacles to the success of the suggestion therapy arise in the form of trauma-based problems, which more than likely date from early childhood. The trauma can be as simple as that when you first attended school your teacher slapped your hand if you used your finger to point to the words as you read.

Our actions are dependent on the information we receive in early life and, therefore, many problems have begun with a 'programme' that was established in early infancy. If you are doing something that you really do not want to do it is because you are acting on an incorrect programme. It is not necessarily bad or good, just inappropriate for you. If a person says to me that he has a problem and he knows exactly when it started—it could be anything from fear of flying to insomnia—invariably he is wrong! Few if any of us is really aware of when or where a trauma started, only when the programme came into operation. The actual trauma will probably have happened much earlier, a later incident only triggering off the programme.

If someone really could remember the trauma, there would not be a problem. The conscious would have been able to deal with the trauma and solve the resulting problem naturally with its logic. The reason the conscious cannot solve the problem—say, fear of flying—is that it does not have all the information it needs to be able to use logic to eliminate the fear.

Sometimes, even trauma-based problems can be treated with suggestion therapy, but there is a higher success rate with problems that are purely and simply bad habits. Most bad habits are not the result of a trauma but rather of practice.

Smoking is a good example of a bad habit. It is only a bad habit once the smoker decides he or she wants to give up.

It might have been an unhealthy habit but it did not start out as a bad one, from the individual's point of view. Humans do not persist at acquiring bad habits, only at habits they want. For example, nail-biting in its early stages might have been done for comfort, just as thumb-sucking or nose-picking all begin innocently enough. There has been extensive research to prove that the nicotine in cigarettes is the reason that smokers find it nearly impossible to quit, although just as many other reports disprove this. In 1992 I was at a conference where figures were produced proving that 90 per cent of smokers gave up without any help from products on the market (including therapy), with 40 per cent of this 90 per cent suffering no ill side-effects whatsoever. The latter tallies with my own statistics. I have a Stop Smoking programme that only takes one hour and carries a very healthy (95 per cent) success rate. The client stops immediately and does not suffer the supposedly mandatory side-effects. Suggestion hypnotherapy that has a positive 30 per cent success rate (and with the right script and hypnotherapist a 60 per cent success rate) has worked for giving up smoking for many years. It is all down to the old rule: 'What the mind expects tends to happen!' If the smoker is programmed to believe there must be side-effects, then there will be. Out of the thousands of smokers I have treated, I have never found a common denominator in the type of side-effect they suffered to give credence to the popular but unproven opinion that smoking is an addiction.

At present there is a great deal of scientific debate over whether smoking is an addiction or a habit. I would say that smoking is a mental addiction, whereas, say, taking heroin is a physical addiction. A mental addiction can be eliminated instantly with hypnosis, without the occurrence of side-effects. On the other hand, a drug addiction takes longer to treat, as the body will necessarily have a physical response when deprived of the drug it has become used to.

There have been extensive tests and surveys by addiction clinics claiming to prove that smoking constitutes a physical addiction to nicotine. But the mere fact that they are called 'addiction' clinics will automatically discourage those smokers who believe it is only a habit. Therefore, the results of any survey based on test results in these clinics are bound to be totally flawed! The belief that smoking is a physical addiction is what the popular nicotine 'patches' trade on. It is hardly surprising that, whatever the manufacturers' claims, their success rate is disappointingly low.

## PROBLEMS AND HYPNOSIS

It always amazes me to see the huge number of weekend courses for the mind that are available in the UK. Unfortunately not all of them are good and some of them are very esoteric. The course 'junkies' tend to be forever taking one course or another, almost every weekend. You can easily spot them. They analyse your conversation and then assess you in public. Life is not as straightforward as this and it soon becomes very boring. I fear we may soon become a nation of DIY health analysts, just acting on theories. Not a very pleasant thought! As a therapist one is are taught to watch out for 'therapy' junkies. These are people who go around the different therapists, trying everything even though their own doctor can find nothing wrong with them. These people never get any better and have either had every illness imaginable or stick to the same one that resists cure no matter whom they see. These people are always difficult to treat because they actually get satisfaction out of the constant attention their problem receives.

If you are going to try your hand at suggestion hypnosis after reading this book, then keep it simple. Do not try to analyse your problem too deeply. If you or someone you are hypnotizing does not respond to suggestion hypnosis, then you will know that more advanced work is needed. At least trying it yourself first will save you the cost of going to a hypnotherapist, who may charge anything between £25 and £150 per session to get the same results you could get at home. Also, the information in this book will help you to know which questions to ask a hypnotherapist so that you can find one with the right training to assist you in more advanced work. If there is some aspect of your behaviour that you want to change, use hypnosis to your advantage—but do not abuse it. If someone else says you have a problem which you have not been aware of and which does not bother you, then it is not your problem—it is theirs! Remember the old saying: 'If it ain't broken, don't fix it.'

## RULES OF THE MIND

There are certain rules that the mind always follows. I have listed below the ones I find are the most interesting and helpful. You do not have to be an expert psychologist to follow them. If you want to use and programme a

computer, you do not need to become a computer expert—
you just need to know the basics for the work you will be
doing. The same applies to the mind. You do not need to
study psychology for years to use suggestion hypnosis;
you just need to know the essentials. Although minds are far
more complex than the most sophisticated computer ever
designed, they all rest on the same basic foundations. The
four rules that follow can help you to understand how you
can work on yourself to achieve changes in your behaviour.

## *Rule 1*

Every thought creates a physical reaction. Research has shown
that emotions, brought on by thought, cause an inward
physical reaction. Worry, for example, causes changes in the
stomach (ulcers, diarrhoea, digestion problems, etc.). Anger
stimulates the adrenal glands, causing increased adrenaline
in the bloodstream affecting many bodily functions. It is better
to vent anger, therefore, than to suppress it. Anxiety and fear
stimulate the blood supply, possibly leading to a high
pulse rate and blood-pressure. The subconscious mind,
too, is affected by thoughts with strong emotional content;
once these have been accepted they become a programme
and trigger the same response over and over again.

## *Rule 2*

You cannot have two conflicting thoughts at one time:
for example, you can be either sad or happy, you cannot be
both at once. You can train yourself to change moods,
however depressing your environment. If you have a

worrying thought you can learn to shelve it and bring forward a memory of a more pleasant occasion. You can make a 'hell out of heaven'. I was living on a beautiful Malaysian island when I began writing this book. Suddenly, out of nowhere, there came a host of problems that brought me depression, even in paradise. One of the wise islanders to whom I remarked: 'There is no peace in paradise' replied: 'The only paradise is in your mind.' How true.

You can also make a 'heaven out of hell'. Take for example the person in jail who still manages to live happily through his imagination and thoughts. One of my students had, many years before, served a six-year jail sentence as a political prisoner. He served his time in the same jail in South Africa as Nelson Mandela and, although the experience was horrendous, he kept his sanity by thinking of beautiful and peaceful surroundings and all the good things in life, remaining positive through the hell to which he was being subjected. When I met him he still had a wonderful outlook on life, which made him very easy to converse with and enabled him to become a very calming therapist. The jail sentence had given him the keen ambition to help people. He has now taken his skills back to Africa.

A negative mind can soon become ill and plummet into the depths of depression if not alleviated. Negativity and depression can be overcome by practising good, positive thoughts. The mind needs 'feeding' through the powers of hearing, vision and speech.

## Hearing
Censor your thoughts to keep them positive. Choose carefully what TV programmes you watch or with whom

you socialize. There is an old saying that your character can be assessed by the company you keep. When I lived and worked in Hollywood a famous old director I was interviewing put it simply, but colourfully, like this: 'When you lie down with dogs you get up with fleas.'

## Vision

Look at pleasant scenery. If possible, travel to the countryside or recall favourite places by looking through photographs. Watch pleasant and light-hearted TV programmes; switch off programmes which disturb you. Select carefully which newspapers you read. 'Pass' on upsetting news that is no use to you. I edited a video trade paper when I lived in Hollywood. This was in 1982, when cable TV was booming in the US while, back in the UK, video machines were first being marketed. I noticed that the levels of violence in the US were very frightening. Television news was full of violence. When it became apparent that video shops and video nasties were coming on the UK market, I predicted in an article that in 10 years' time the UK would have changed out of all recognition, having itself become a very violent society. I fear that my prediction has come true.

## Speech

Speak positively and you will begin to see the changes in other people's attitudes towards you. Change negative ideas to positive ones and you will find yourself becoming more popular with positive people. Negative people will only hold back your growth. Suppose you were to go into a wine bar and see a group of people in a corner enjoying themselves, all talking positively and generating a feeling of enthusiasm.

Now imagine a negative person joining the group. He or she would easily make the crowd feel uncomfortable, affecting their confidence, possibly introducing depressing conversation and sapping their enthusiasm even further. On the other hand, if there were a group of moaners in the wine bar with negative attitudes and a positive person were to join them, more than likely the opposite would occur. The solitary, positive person would be brought down to feeling negative in a very short time.

It is easy to slip into negative thinking. The ill mind is far more susceptible to negative thoughts, resulting in deep depression. When I have a client who is in deep depression, I advise him to start to monitor what he sees, hears and says, just as I am advising you now. Your brain is fed through these three faculties, so feed them correctly. This in turn will change your attitudes. To many people it comes as quite a surprise to realize that they have a choice as to whether they want to think positively or be depressive. It is even more unsettling to them when they realize that they can train themselves to take control of their thoughts and be the master of their mind instead of its servant. There is a difference between suppressing emotions and moving them. Suppressing is when you push an emotion down and bury it. Moving an emotion allows it to be accessible when you are ready to deal with it yourself.

I interviewed Uri Geller, the incredible fellow who became famous by bending keys and other metal through the power of his mind. I could not have been more impressed with his vast house, his personality and his many photographs of his beautiful family. On the face of it— and I have no reason to believe otherwise—he is living proof of what visualization can do. He told me how he used a television screen in his mind to visualize how he wanted to feel, using his imagination to invent his own movie, showing what he wanted to achieve, his goals, eliminating negative thoughts and spurring a host of other equally positive assignments. He takes the time to make it work.

Pictures are the language the subconscious understands. If you picture yourself happy, your subconscious will send you happy thoughts. If you picture yourself a failure, your subconscious, thinking that is what you want to be, will send you all the reasons you need to fail so that you can attain what it believes is your goal. In Uri Geller's early days he performed stage hypnosis and was well aware of the power of the mind. He knew that you control your mind, not the other way round. Unfortunately, most people let their mind control them, looking on helplessly as it takes over. It is very difficult to get the average person to accept the simple fact that he is in charge of his own destiny.

Probably from early childhood, training and remarks like: 'I am only human!'—said as if it were an apology—have given we humans a subconscious feeling of inferiority. The same words said with confidence and determination have a completely different meaning. Try putting a silent thought after the words: 'I am only human (I do not make mistakes)'.

## The Box Therapy
This is a technique very similar to using a mental TV screen to remove unwanted thoughts or experiences running through your mind. For example, we have all at some time been waiting for a telephone call that will bring the information needed so that we can make a particular

decision and act on it. It could be as simple as whether we get a rise or as serious as whether to accept a job abroad. Knowing the telephone call is a day away, many hours can be wasted running over in your mind a list of 'What ifs?' This is a very time-consuming exercise and, after the first run of 'What ifs?', serves no useful purpose. Sadly, this does not stop us from doing it. The mind has been excited, which has caused it to race.

People who are depressed have minds that are racing constantly, going over all the things that have gone wrong. Tranquillizers are often prescribed by doctors to slow down the mind and rest it. But the drugs do not treat the cause, just the symptom. The Box Technique is a natural way to help you to shut out any depressing, unproductive thought:

Visualize the thought and use your imagination to build a box. Picture the size, the colour, what the box is made of, etc. Put a door in it.
Place the negative thought into the box. Close the door to the box and lock it, then take out the key and put it away safe.
Now, immediately replace the thought with another, positive one. Something you want to think of.
If an unwanted thought or the old one comes back, repeat the box routine and replace the bad thought with a good one.

You can train yourself to do this and it works if you persevere. You need to work at it—it does not just happen, as if by magic.

## *Rule 3*

Imagination replaces reason: or 'What the mind expects tends to happen.' The imagination can be so intense. A thought, although unfounded, can occasionally lead even to murder—often called a crime of passion. The image in the subconscious can be so powerful that someone in its grip is unable to reason logically. Violence would be unheard of if logic were to override the emotional response. The mental image becomes fact and is like a blueprint. Worrying can elicit a picture of what *might* happen, even if this outcome is unlikely or even impossible when considered logically. Expecting ill health or bad luck can create it. Superstitious beliefs ignore any positive alternatives.

Once an idea has been accepted by the subconscious, it remains there until replaced by another idea. The longer the idea remains, the more opposition to change there is. Habits, whether good or bad, are formed consciously. If you put a three-foot plank on the floor you can easily walk across it. But if you put it between two high buildings, each of many storeys, you will have extreme difficulty walking across, due to your imagination taking over and questions popping into your mind causing doubt, the most obvious one being: 'What would happen if I were to fall?' First comes the thought and then the action. The thought always comes first.

We have habits of both thought and action. To change our actions we must change our thoughts. This takes work. It can be done quickly by hypnosis or slowly by perseverance. You have to practise your way out of a habit. An immediate change can only be achieved by persuading the subconscious, in hypnosis, that this action is no longer appropriate.

## *Rule 4*

If an individual condition lasts long enough it will cause physical change. Research shows that 70 per cent of ailments are not caused by a particular organ of the body going wrong but by emotional activity attacking and weakening it. The organ is disturbed by the reaction of the nervous system to negative ideas held in the subconscious mind. Our state of mind is relative to our immune system. We are a mind in a body and one needs the other to function efficiently.

The greater the conscious effort, the less the subconscious response. This can be proved when a person is trying to remember a place or name. The more the conscious effort, the more difficult it is to remember. But when the thought is changed, the answer comes forward—when there is no pressure.

For example, how many times have you tried hard to sleep only to find yourself more and more awake? Or tried hard to relax and become more tense? It is only when you ease the pressure on yourself that your subconscious can come to the fore.

## HOW IMPORTANT IS VISUALIZATION?

In order to be successful at what you want to do, you need to have a goal or vision. 'I want to be happy' is not specific enough. Set your goals in detail, give your subconscious something to go for. So, be specific: visualize what you want and then set out to get it. The tools are at hand in this book. Your tools are words—the correct words. Words said in normal consciousness may be edited out by that sophisticated computer in your mind because of an earlier programme which may be locked on to a trauma you are not even aware of. In order for you to accept new ideas, you have to start to reprogramme your mind so that it is in a position to accept new thoughts. Then the changes are immediate or, as the Bible says, 'in the blinking of an eye'.

Be careful what you wish for—you may get it! If you have not specified in detail what you want, then you may be in for a disappointment. Your dreams may have already been granted without you realizing it.

I decided to do a test recently after re-reading one of my favourite books, *Think and Get Rich* by Napoleon Hill. I visualized something simple I needed. It was an overnight travel bag. I was in Malaysia writing this book and I was asked to do a lecture on stopping smoking which involved an overnight stay. I only had large luggage cases with me, so I imagined having a travel case. I did not visualize the shape or the colour, just thought of a travel bag. It was an unlikely object to appear. When I arrived for my lecture, I had packed my overnight things in my briefcase and in a small, indiscreet carrier bag. The lecture went well and I was treated to lunch by the chairman of the company. At the end, I was presented with a gift. Somehow, I knew what it was before I opened it—sure enough, an overnight travel bag! Not my favourite colour or shape, but a travel bag none the less. Next time I shall have to practise what I preach and be more specific and detailed with my visualization!

After using this visualization technique regularly you may find that you can develop it and notice some positive changes. What is happening is that you have instructed your subconscious by visualization, which is the language of the subconscious, as to what you want. The subconscious then sets out to attain it. If there are any telepathic waves to be picked up—which I have always believed in—the chances are that when you test this idea you will see a lot of change for the better.

Your subconscious is actively working on acquiring your goals in more ways than you can possibly imagine. Positive thinking and visualization are vital.

# three

# SELF-HYPNOSIS

---

A ll hypnosis is really self-hypnosis. Hypnotherapists are merely the guides who can help subjects into hypnosis, making it more likely that they will enter a good, deep trance state quickly and easily. Having said this, generally when people talk about self-hypnosis they mean putting oneself into hypnosis without anyone else's aid.

Stage hypnotists have developed certain inductions which can put a person instantly into hypnosis. The induction takes only seconds, but these techniques are not 100 per cent reliable and are generally only successful on suggestible people, who usually make up approximately a third of any given audience. Stage hypnotists are particularly experienced in such instant induction techniques because time is of the essence in their act, lest the audience gets bored or restless.

On the other hand, hypnotherapists enjoy the luxury of time and can choose the induction they prefer, whether it be rapid or slow and relaxing. They are more likely to take the slower approach, considering they will be treating both the susceptible and the not-so-susceptible subject. Hypnotherapists know that everyone can be induced into hypnosis, yet they would usually rather be sure of achieving good hypnosis with the slow technique than chance losing the subject's belief structure at the beginning of therapy with the not-as-successful rapid or instant techniques.

At one time in the early, experimental days of hypnosis (as far back as the 1800s) Esdaile, one of the pioneers of hypnosis, would take up to an hour and a half to induce deep trance for anaesthesia. Modern hypnotherapists, with more understanding of how the mind works, have been able to speed up the inductions and have a choice of three types ranging from only seconds in length to 20 minutes, depending on preference.

So really we are dealing with percentages when we talk of inductions. The instant induction needs a very confident hypnotist and a suggestible subject. The rapid induction works on a larger percentage of people than the instant, while the progressive, slow method is far more reliable. Stage hypnotists know they will be able to work with approximately one third of the audience using instant inductions. Hypnotherapists know they can work with 100 per cent of their subjects as long as they take the necessary time each individual requires.

Self-hypnosis, on the other hand, has a lot of hurdles to get over which, if not prepared for, prevent some subjects feeling any relaxation at all, whatever induction they use. Subjects must be made aware of these obstacles; a basic understanding of how the mind works (see Chapter 2) will be of great benefit to anyone who may, or who has, found it difficult to go into hypnosis.

The first major obstacle is that there is no feeling in hypnosis, just as there is no feeling when you go into a daydream. So how do you know when you are hypnotized? The fact is, you don't! You may have seen people in a hypnosis stage show perform extraordinary tasks and who then, when brought out of trance, refuse to believe they were in hypnosis at all. Just as the alcoholic has to admit he is an alcoholic before he can be treated, the person who is going to practise self-hypnosis needs to accept that it is unlikely that he will have any feeling in hypnosis except that of relaxation.

The exception is when the subconscious may have taken a suggestion on board from something read or heard earlier about hypnosis. This may cause some feeling or a tingling sensation, which the subconscious 'expects' to feel when in hypnosis. The subject may not have any memory of hearing this information but it presents itself when he is hypnotized. It was once common practice for hypnotists to suggest this to a subject as a suggestibility test. The subject who said he felt a slight tingling had accepted the suggestion and therefore was suggestible. The person feeling nothing had not accepted the suggestion but could still be experiencing the same quality of hypnosis.

## How Do You Hypnotize Yourself?

In order to hypnotize yourself (or someone else) you need three basic scripts (all found in this book). The three steps to hypnotherapy are:

1. Induction script (see pages 57–60)
   ('Deepeners' (see pages 60–6) can be used before the suggestion for deeper relaxation)
2. Suggestion script (see Chapter 4)

3. Counting out of hypnosis (see page 70)

## METHODS OF INDUCTION

There are three types of induction used to relax a person into hypnosis. In order of extremes they are: shock (instant induction), confusion (rapid induction) and boredom (progressive induction).

I have purposely excluded instructions for the instant and rapid inductions because they are more advanced techniques; I mention them briefly now only so that you know they exist.

### *Instant Induction*

The instant induction, which has a shock element and is immediate, looks very impressive for demonstrations, taking only seconds to induce full relaxation. It can be as dramatic as the hypnotist grabbing a subject by the head, shoulders or arms and barking out the order: 'Sleep!'

Instant induction is used mainly by hypnotists in the US and is quite spectacular to witness. It can be used on anyone, although in the UK some people do not like this type of induction and feel threatened merely by seeing a demonstration of it. The subject may look as if he has gone into a faint but is fully aware and finds it pleasant and relaxing. It is very effective, demonstrating the power of suggestion at its best. If a person has experienced a severe trauma or scare, he will be automatically in hypnosis. The conscious mind stops processing and the subconscious is vulnerable. This induction needs another person to act as hypnotist and cannot be used for self-hypnosis.

## Rapid Induction

The rapid induction, which basically confuses the mind, overloading it, presents a more gentle approach but still takes less than a minute to induce.

The American Dave Elman, a modern master of hypnosis, had developed a method of rapid induction which uses confusion and complicated short instructions to close down the conscious part of the mind, thus exposing the subconscious. It is very effective and this type of induction is useful for inducing hypnosis once a person has already experienced hypnosis before. As with instant induction, this method needs another to perform the hypnosis and so in unsuitable for self-hypnosis.

## Progressive Induction

The progressive induction really bores the mind into hypnosis. It is considered the most reliable and is the one normally used for self-hypnosis. This traditional, progressive method can take quite some time—the one illustrated in this chapter (pages 57–60) takes approximately 10 minutes, if read slowly and soothingly.

You need not have another person present to guide you into hypnosis; you can just listen to a recording, either bought or pre-recorded by yourself. It is an exercise into relaxation, using many different words to entice a reaction and partic-ipation. For instance, the hypnosis 'script' as it is called, may suggest: 'Tighten the muscles in your feet.' The instructions thus occupy the conscious while relaxing the mind, allowing the suggestion to be accepted. As the instructions become monotonous, the mind responds even more.

Because it is more effective at least to have a modicum of attention while inducing the relaxation, it is better to have a script with varied words. It is not as effective to keep using the same verb continuously in the instructions, e.g.: 'Tighten the muscles in your feet....now relax those muscles. Tighten the muscles in your calves....now relax those muscles,' etc.

There are exceptions to this rule, however, in that certain words may be used continually to join different parts of the suggestion together. 'Now' can be used liberally, as can powerful words such as 'down' which, used repetitively, lead the subject deeper into trance.

The progressive relaxation technique gradually slows down the metabolism of the subject and so, however stressed or tense he may be at the beginning, eventually this technique will guide him into deep relaxation. The technique ensures that the sufficient amount of relaxation is reached in order for the subject to then followed the appropriate suggestion and, as long as the problem being tackled is not trauma-based and is in the subject's interest, the subconscious will accept the new programming.

You can prevent yourself going into hypnosis by refusing to relax. Other than this there is no reason why a suggestion should not work. Do not spend time worrying whether you are achieving hypnosis. Just let your mind drift with the words and it will happen.

# METHODS OF LEARNING SELF-HYPNOSIS

First, you must accept that you can be hypnotized, that it is nothing to do with intelligence or willpower. It is a fact that we can all hypnotize ourselves. If you are not succeeding, it is your responsibility. Like everything else, practice makes perfect. In order to have really good self-hypnosis, I would suggest you ask a volunteer—a partner or friend perhaps—to guide you. Then, when you have been guided into trance, it will be much easier for you to produce the same results for yourself at another time.

To help you understand the difficulties I would like you to imagine that you are a native of Barbados and that you are watching television. You have never experienced severe cold or seen snow. You are watching a film showing a group of people stranded in a snowstorm. Their car has broken down and they are suffering with cold and frostbite. They are not prepared or dressed properly and so are exposed to the elements. If you had never experienced the intense cold of a snowstorm it would be impossible for someone to explain it so that you could actually feel it and experience the effects of extreme cold.

If you were then taken to Britain and experienced a cold day, this still would not give you an insight into what snow feels like and how cold the climate can become in a blizzard. But suppose you were taken to the Arctic in a blizzard and you had first-hand experience of what this type of cold was like in relation to the cold you had already been subjected to. When you returned to the sunshine and warmth of Barbados, the next time you saw a film of a snowstorm you would know exactly how it felt. You might even spontaneously shiver at just the image or thought of it.

Once your mind has experienced a feeling it is permanently stored in the memory banks. Therefore, your memory can immediately remind you of such experiences. A favourite song can bring a sadness or joy, a particular smell can also awaken a memory in a split second.

In terms of hypnosis, if you first try it yourself with just your own meditations or with a selection of the many cassette tapes or videos, you risk not getting anywhere near the true experience, like the Barbadian watching the snow blizzard who has no idea what it feels like to be really cold and who cannot figure out what all the fuss is about. If you approach self-hypnosis knowing what to expect, or rather what not to expect, with practice and perseverance there is no reason why you cannot use this incredible control of your own mind to change your attitudes and personality defects. It is that powerful.

Also, once you have experienced hypnosis with a helpful guide you can easily attain it by yourself if you have been given some good instructions into hypnosis and methods to help you, especially if this includes a post-hypnotic suggestion (see below). Even with all this extra help, however, you need to practise self-hypnosis continually. If you do not you will find, as the old saying goes, that 'what you don't use, you lose!'

The reason so many people are disappointed by self-hypnosis tapes or videos is that they expect to feel hypnotized, even to the extent of expecting to be in a coma-like state. Once you have been hypnotized the tapes and videos can be very beneficial, although no more so than creating your own tape recordings from something as simple as a pocket recorder and creating your own personal scripts from the rules for suggestions given in Chapter 4.

There are four methods by which you can learn about and try self-hypnosis. I have listed them below, together with their disadvantages. There is no question about it, for speed and depth of relaxation it is to your advantage to have someone to help guide you for your first hypnosis experience.

## Method One: Enlisting a Volunteer to Help You

The advantages of this method are that the volunteer can be guided by this book and, if he follows the scripts carefully, he will induce good, deep hypnosis. In order to produce a deep trance all you need is suggestion hypnosis. That is to say, anyone you feel comfortable with can read the words and you will go into hypnosis.

The disadvantages of this will be the attitude or personality of the volunteer you have chosen. He or she may be a giggler; likewise choosing an unconfident stutterer would be very distracting. Ideally your guide should be someone with a calm, pleasant and articulate voice.

## Method Two: Using a Pre-recorded Professional Tape or Video

With perseverance this can be quite a helpful method. Try to make sure there are as few distractions as possible: disconnect the phone, for example, and try to keep your mind off daily routines or planning what you will be having for dinner; instead, listen to and play close attention to the tape or video. At first you may find it difficult to relax enough to obtain a good deep trance, but with practice you will achieve some sort of relaxation.

One disadvantage of this method is that you do not have someone to guide you or to use deepeners (see below) that encourage a much deeper state of trance. Nor do you have someone there to pace the hypnosis to your individual thoughts.

Another disadvantage is that tapes and videos cannot take into account the fact that something may distract you, so you can easily become 'out-of-sync' with the induction at the beginning stages of hypnosis. Struggling and worrying that you cannot then 'catch up' interfere with the relaxation and with your chance of achieving good hypnosis.

## Method Three: Learning with an Experienced Hypnotherapist

The advantage is that the hypnotherapist will have the expertise to sound confident, although he or she will only be following scripts similar to those outlined in this book. There is no reason why a volunteer cannot induce the same quality of hypnosis as an experienced hypnotherapist. For suggestion hypnosis only, an experienced hypnotherapist is not a necessity. For advanced techniques an experienced hypnotherapist is essential. Not because these techniques are dangerous—they are not—but mainly because without the necessary competence it will be difficult for an untrained volunteer to work efficiently and easily.

I have trained hypnotherapists in workshops who have

read every conceivable book on the workings of hypnosis but who, before the course, did not have the confidence to carry out the advanced techniques needed to create a change of behaviour in their clients. After the all-important one-to-one training, their confidence was established. For a student to try and learn advanced techniques in hypnosis from books alone would be like going for a solo flight in a light aircraft without ever having any hands-on experience. That is, it can be done but it takes absolute confidence and guts and when it comes to the crunch not everyone is cut out for it.

The main disadvantage of this method is the cost. An experienced hypnotherapist, performing suggestion hypnosis only, will cost you anything between £25 and £150 per session and he or she will only be working with a script similar to those in Chapter 4. Anyone who can read the appropriate scripts in a confident and easy manner can attain the same level of hypnosis as the professional hypnotherapist, without the extra cost.

## Method Four: Group Instruction

This is quite popular and courses range in length from half a day to a full weekend, depending on the technique used and what the course covers. The main disadvantages are that group instruction is sometimes costly and not always effective.

# PROGRESSIVE INDUCTION

You can choose scripts that take you by the sea, to a garden, on a boat or on a magical journey—your imagination is the limit. I have found that the garden visualization is soothing to most people, and therefore have used it in the sample script below.

To help you read aloud the script with the correct pauses, I have purposely exaggerated the spacing. It is also important to realize that the grammar does not have to be precise nor the words arranged accurately. In fact, the more 'inaccurate' the better, as this causes a controlled confusion in the subject's mind.

The scripted instructions that follow are for the volunteer who is guiding a subject into self-hypnosis. If you do not know anyone who can act as your guide, then tape yourself on a tape recorder and play the script back to yourself *while you are sitting or lying down comfortably.*

## Progressive Relaxation Induction Script

'*I want you to imagine that you're checking your body to ensure you become totally relaxed.....as your muscles relax, just let your mind relax also.....begin with your feet.....feel your toes.....stretch them, feel the texture of what your feet are resting on.....begin to tighten your calves.....now relax them.....let that relaxation spread past your ankles, up your calves to the back of the knee.....feel those muscles easing.....resting comfortable.....now your thighs, pull them tight.....be aware of those long muscles tensing.....now relax those muscles.....feel them lengthening and resting comfortably.....feel your legs as they sink even deeper into the cushions as you relax even more.....now your stomach* muscles, pull them together gently.....now let them expand and relax comfortably.

'Your shoulders and back muscles.....flex your shoulders.....feel those muscles pull across your back.....now let your shoulders slouch as you relax the muscles.....and notice how your spine sinks deeper into your chair, as you relax even more deeply.....notice how easy and regular your breathing has become. Now your fingertips and fingers, clench them, feel that tension.....now relax them.....and allow the relaxation to spread up your arms to your neck. Make sure your neck is comfortable with your head in an easy position.....tighten up your neck muscles.....now let them loosen up.....as the muscles relax, allow your neck to back into a comfortable position. Your face muscles are flat and stretch comfortably across your face.....squeeze up your face and feel the tension.....now relax those muscles and feel them lengthening and softening, relax more than ever before.

'You can now feel the air temperature against your skin.....it feels smooth and comfortable.....now you can allow the relaxation to reach your scalp, knowing that you are relaxed throughout your body from the top of your head to the tips of your toes. Your body is now loose.....and limp.....and heavy.....and relaxed.....notice how your body is sinking deeper into relaxation.....as your breathing becomes more regular and easy. In a moment I will count slowly from one.....to 10.......and with each number you drift deeper and deeper into peaceful relaxation. 1...2...3...4...5...6...7...8...9...10 [count slowly and deliberately].

'You are now feeling so deeply relaxed.....you find it easy to focus your attention, and imagine things very clearly.....and I want you to imagine that you are standing on a balcony which has steps leading down to a beautiful garden.....as you look into the garden, you see that it is surrounded with lovely trees ensuring the garden is private, secluded and peaceful. There are flower beds set in the lovely lawn and further along is a waterfall flowing into a stream.....listen to the sound of the water.....as you look around, you see the trees and you hear a faint sound of a bird in the distance, adding to the feeling of deep relaxation through your entire being.

'If you look more closely you will see that there are five steps leading down to the garden and then a small path that leads to the waterfall. In a moment we will walk down the steps and with each step you go deeper and deeper into relaxation. So let's begin.....watch your foot as you place it onto the first step.....and as you do this, you feel yourself going deeper into relaxation. [As you lead your subject down the steps you find you can slow down the rhythm of his or her breathing by slowing down the pace of the descent]. Down onto the second step and as you feel your foot firmly placed on the step, you feel a wonderful relief as you drift even deeper into relaxation. Down onto the third step, feeling wonderfully free and.....so.....so.....relaxed. As your foot reaches for the fourth step, another wave of relaxation drifts through your whole body. Down onto the fifth step now and feeling even more deeply relaxed than ever before. Now you are standing on the lawn.....you see a little way ahead is the waterfall and at the side of it is a garden bench.....notice the colour of the bench.....what it is made of.....[If this is being read, add: 'Say "yes" when you see the bench in your mind'—make sure you have done the 'Are You Visual?' test on page 17, Chapter 1 before the hypnosis].

'In a moment I would like you to walk over to the bench.....and sit down on the bench.....When you sit down you will be surprised at how comfortable it is.....and then you will be even more relaxed than you are now.....so let's begin to walk over.....now sit down on the bench.....as you sit down on the bench, take a deep breath.....and as you *breathe out you feel a wave of relaxation go through your body relaxing every muscle and nerve......[stay silent for the count of three seconds]......as you breathe in......you breathe in positive thoughts......and as you breathe out......you breathe out negative thoughts......leaving room for more positive thoughts.'*

To deepen the level of relaxation an extra script, called a deepener, is used when the subject is in hypnosis. The progressive induction can be followed by one of the deepeners below. I favour the fantasy garden, but either the ruler or the lift are just as satisfactory.

The above induction should be followed by the self-hypnosis script given later in this chapter or by any suggestion that is appropriate.

## DEEPENERS

### *What Is A Deepener?*

A deepener is a suggestion given while the subject is in hypnosis for the purpose of attaining a deeper trance. The words used suggest that you will go deeper into hypnosis and various exercises allow the imagination to take the mind to an even deeper level of relaxation. The purpose of this is so the subject can completely relax, slowing down conscious thoughts, allowing suggestions to be accepted easily without too much interference from the logical, conscious part of the mind.

The deep trance does not have many benefits in therapy, apart from when there is a need to be anaesthetized. But it is a wonderful feeling to attain in self-hypnosis, very comforting and secure. It also helps you to focus your imagination better.

The main purpose of a deepener is to guide the subject into a feeling of concentrated, pure relaxation—an added advantage is that it shows subjects how they can adjust the level of relaxation themselves.

## How to Use a Deepener

There are four examples of deepeners listed below which have been used and tested for many years in relaxation techniques. While a person is in hypnosis the subconscious is accessible. Therefore, any instruction followed by the words, 'and you will be five times more relaxed,' or 'and then you will be doubly more relaxed' will be a deepener. An example of a simple deepener would be to say 'In a moment when I snap my fingers you will be doubly relaxed,' or 'When I drop your arm into your lap you will be five times more relaxed.'

Stage hypnotists use this technique both to entertain the audience and to deepen the subject. They may say: 'When I touch my ear you will go into a deep sleep,' and the subject immediately mimics a deep sleep. In fact, the subject is aware of everything going on but the subconscious is now in charge. It takes words literally and, therefore, is very precise in the actions it performs. If the subconscious is requested—as can happen with stage hypnotists—to act like a chicken, the subconscious will go into the memory banks and the person will do an excellent imitation of a chicken. Normally the subject would be far too inhibited to do this consciously. But the subconscious has accessed the memory files, enabling the subject to give a brilliant performance.

When the hypnotist touches his or her ear, the subject goes directly into what looks like a deep sleep. The subconscious has accepted the instruction and followed it without the participant being aware of no longer being consciously in control. Remember, the stage hypnotist has checked the audience for suggestibility and will be using only those who are very suggestible, simply for speed and entertainment value.

Hypnotherapist use deepeners to help subjects into deep relaxation, so as to enable the subject to experience a sense of total calm. This technique is especially effective with high-powered business people.

Four deepeners—the lift, the ruler, a visualization deepener and steps into paradise—are given below.

## The Lift

This is an old favourite that has been used for years. I used it for the first few years of my practice but later came to prefer the ruler or the steps into paradise.

*'I would like you to come with me into a lift.....the doors are opening and you step inside.....it's roomy and feels comfortable.....look around the lift.....it's a very special lift.....notice the colour of the surroundings.....a comfortable soft colour that reassures you.....from the panel on one side of the doors that are now closing you notice that we are on the 3rd floor.....you look at the panel again and see that the lift is going down to the 2nd floor.....look.....it has now reached the 2nd floor and the lift door opens.....but you do not want to get out because you know you can go deeper into*

*the basement of relaxation.....so look for the button that says Floor 1.....when you are ready, press that button.....we now start to drift.....floating down to the basement of relaxation.....so look for the button that says "B".....press the button and notice that the lift goes down.....and down.....bypassing the first floor.....and deeper and deeper.....down to the very basement of relaxation. Down, down, now you are at the basement.....so relaxed.....so calm.....so free.....the doors open and you walk out into a wonderful, luxurious, comfortable place.....there is a chair that looks so relaxing you walk over to sit on the chair.....knowing you will sink into the cushions.....and as you do so you experience a marvellous feeling of pure peace of mind and tranquility.'*

## *The Ruler*

This is a wonderful deepener. It allows the subject to have full control of the level of the trance. It is particularly useful for the person who has a fear of hypnosis.

*'What I would like you to do is imagine a three-foot ruler in front of you. This is a very special ruler because it measures relaxation. [If this is being read aloud by a friend, he or she should add: 'Say "yes" when you see it.'] Good. What colour is it? [Wait for a response.] Good. Now if you look more closely you will see there are numbers on this ruler. At the very top you can see a number 1 and at the bottom you are surprised to see the numbers go right down to 100. In a few moments I will count from 1 to 3 and snap my fingers, and when I do a number will appear as if by magic. This number will indicate your level of relaxation. 1...2...3...[snap fingers]. What*

*number do you see? [Wait for a response.] Good. Now take*
*a deep breath and every time I ask you to do this you*
*will find that you become twice as relaxed as you are*
*now. Taking another deep breath, breathe in. Good. Now*
*breathe out slowly. What number is on your ruler now?'*

What is amazing about this ruler deepener is that you can
actually determine your own relaxation by picking a
number and going straight there. I will show you what I
mean...

*'What I want you to do is look at the ruler and go up to*
*number 5.....now drag your eyes down.....down to number*
*25.....feel yourself going deeper and deeper into*
*relaxation.....now drag your eyes further down the ruler*
*towards number 50.....feel yourself being pulled into a*
*wonderful, peaceful relaxation.....now drag your eyes*
*down to number 90.....notice how deeply relaxed you feel*
*as you drag your eyes down the ruler. Go down and down*
*the ruler, pulling yourself into a wonderful, deep, peaceful,*
*feeling. Now, slowly come up the ruler and notice how much*
*lighter you feel as you float up.'*

At this point you can either bring the subject out of
hypnosis by counting him back up or take him down to the
basement (100) and give him a suggestion.

### Visualization Deepener

This type of deepener is for people who can visualize
easily.

*'As you sit there enjoying the feeling of relaxation and*
*allowing yourself to go easily and effortlessly into rest, I*

*would like you to visualize yourself in a place that you have enjoyed visiting, where you have felt happy, calm and relaxed.....allow yourself to be in that place now.....take in the security.....notice the colours around you.....how bright, how dull, how soft, how pleasing. Take in the atmosphere.....notice if there is a breeze and whether there is sun or shade.....as you allow yourself to remember this pleasant memory, so you go deeper and deeper into complete and utter rest.'*

## Steps into Paradise

This deepener is my favourite for exercising depth in preparation for self-hypnosis. First you guide the subject onto the garden bench (see the progressive relaxation script, above), then continue with this deepener.

*'As you are sitting comfortably, you see a little way ahead 10 steps that lead to a lower part of the garden.....and you can see just a few feet in front of the bottom step a large heavy wooden door.....set in an archway made out of stone that leads to another part of the garden.....you don't know what it is like through the door but you have this feeling that it is a wonderful, peaceful place.....you feel the need to explore and so you decide to walk down the steps.....you know instinctively that each step will bring a feeling of deep relaxation.....you walk over to the top steps and as you begin to descend on the first step, a wonderful feeling of relaxation comes over you.....the next step and you feel you are going deeper and deeper into relaxation.....down.....to the third step, even deeper relaxed.....the fourth step, deeper still.....down to the fifth.....the sixth.....and the seventh.....feeling deeper and deeper relaxed.....you are nearly at the bottom now.....the eighth*

*step.....you are feeling so, so relaxed.....the ninth and the tenth.....you begin to walk over to the doorway, knowing that on the other side is the most beautiful place.....your special place.....as you put your hand on the large handle, the door creaks open and you are confronted with the most beautiful view.*

*'What makes this place so special is that you can add whatever you like, whether it be mountains, sand or flowers.....you look around and you design your special place.....you know that this is the basement of your relaxation and that you can come here at any time, to address your subconscious or just to relax.....you see a comfortable place to sit.....you can even lie down if you wish.....you walk over and make yourself comfortable and as you do, a feeling of pure peace of mind and a deep relaxation washes over you like a wave and both your body and mind are in complete harmony, totally relaxed.....as you relax your mind, it re-energizes itself, your body allowing your own healing forces to function.'*

## Post-Hypnotic Suggestion for Self-Hypnosis

Once you have established a deep, relaxed trance, you/the subject are now ready for a post-hypnotic suggestion. This is a suggestion in the form of an instruction, to be acted on when the subject has terminated the trance and his or her conscious mind has taken over again. It is powerful and remarkable. The subconscious activates the instruction without the subject's conscious being aware that the suggestion was ever made in the first place.

I find this method most effective as an instruction. It has

a jolt and trigger effect. This means that the instruction includes an action, for example an arm dropping into the lap. The trigger of the drop or jolt keeps the conscious focused and occupied, allowing the suggestion to be fully accepted by the subconscious. This is much more effective when a person has been in hypnosis at least three times, taking care each time to guide the subject to a deeper level of relaxation. For a post-hypnotic suggestion to work, it is important to take the trouble to do the important preliminary exercises into deep trance.

### The Post-Hypnotic Suggestion (While the Subject Is in Deep Hypnosis)

'In a moment I will ask you to lift up your right arm and silently say the words: "I'm going into deep hypnosis now." As you say the word "hypnosis", let your right arm drop into your lap and you will be even more deeply relaxed than you already are.' [Follow this instruction. Now go to your garden bench and use a deepener—your ruler or fantasy garden. If you use the Ruler Method, check what level of relaxation you are in and then go down to the level you desire. If it is the basement level, say 'basement.']

Before you go into hypnosis, give yourself a time limit and your body will automatically come out of this deep state at the time ordained. Your body has its own clock that keeps perfect time. If you are helping someone with hypnosis, ask him or her to rehearse this time limit while in hypnosis, then bring the subject out of hypnosis and ask him or her to practise in front of you.

It is important to note that if the practice is then done daily, by the end of the week you should be able to imagine the actions (such as your arm falling), like a rehearsal in your mind. After practising for a further week you will be able to do this without even closing your eyes—even on a bus or tube, etc. Like any habit, it needs continual practice. If you stop practising, then the level of relaxation will be lighter. But if kept up, the advantages are tremendous and it only takes a couple of minutes daily.

## ADVANTAGES OF SELF-HYPNOSIS

Here are just four important obvious advantages. There are many more.

1. A deep relaxation in body and mind can be a supplement to someone who is unable to have a full quota of sleep. This method of relaxation can also help a person with insomnia—and is definitely more interesting than counting sheep!
2. Deep relaxation relieves stress immediately.
3. Relaxation can be used to access the subconscious and find information or answer a question that has been bothering you, such as: 'Why am I doing such and such?' The reply will be from the subconscious and it will be correct. If you do not like the answer, you must still accept it, nevertheless. Do not go for a 'best out of three'-type answer. It will not be the right one! Your first answer is always the correct one, because your subconscious never lies.

4. If you want to formulate a speech, you can access your subconscious to do so and leave it to do the work while you get on with something else. Your subconscious has the facility to do this. Unfortunately we do not realize this and do not always trust our subconscious.

Lawyers use this facility in their courtroom speeches, even if they don't always realize it. They have to evaluate new information immediately and build it into their most important closing speech. This skill determines whether someone is simply a good attorney or a brilliant one. And, while they may believe that it is their own skill that they are trusting, it is in fact their subconscious.

## Accessing Your Subconscious in Self-Hypnosis

You should learn to ask questions of your subconscious while you are in hypnosis, when you reach your special place or basement of relaxation. Imagine a TV screen in your mind, about three foot high, and address your questions to that screen. Imagine that the TV screen is your subconscious. Whatever thought comes into your mind when you have asked your question, whether it comes in the form of an image on the screen or just as a word, this is the answer from your subconscious. Do not attempt to analyse the answer.

At first, practise simple questions, such as 'Why am I having trouble sleeping?' (if that is your problem), or: 'Why am I getting so many colds?' Learn to trust your subconscious. (There is more about using self-hypnosis to overcome specific problems in Chapter 4.)

## COUNTING OUT OF HYPNOSIS

You can choose to count yourself out of hypnosis, using whatever combination of numbers you prefer. I like to count out backwards from 10 to 1:

> *'In a moment I will count 10 to 1.....and at the count of one you will open your eyes.....and feel fully aware and enthusiastic.....10...9...8...coming up now.....7...6...5.....more and more aware.....4...3...2...1...eyes open.'*

## DIFFERENT STAGES OF TRANCE

For suggestion hypnosis, any of the stages of trance—from light to quite deep—is adequate. It is only when, acting as a guide, you require the subject to participate in the therapy—perhaps by answering a question or lifting an arm—and find that he or she does not respond that you might misunderstand what is happening and worry that 'something has gone wrong'. There is no need for this worry, as the following explanations of the different stages of trance (including the so-called 'coma' trance) will illustrate.

There are, of course, varying degrees of trance, encouraging different sets of responses. For explanation purposes I have called these stages 'depths'.

## 1. The Light Trance

The light trance is when the mind and body are relaxed enough to slow the mind down so that it can focus in imagination clearly. In this form of trance you can work easily with both suggestion and more advanced therapy. You can even achieve partial amnesia, as the subjects of stage hypnotists often do. The light trance is excellent for accelerated learning. Your conscious is not battling with the new material, logically analysing the new information. The conscious sits back and allows this fresh data to flow through without resistance.

There are certain physical changes that occur when a person is in hypnosis, such as the eyelids rapidly fluttering and the face looking 'droopy', as in sleep. If you instruct the subject to open his or her eyes, the whites of the eyes can look very pink for a second or so due to the relaxation of the eye muscles. There is a list of signs but because they can be very misleading, and because the subject may not show any of these outward signs of being hypnotized while still in deep hypnosis, I have mentioned them only so that you are aware of their existence.

## 2. Somnambulism

The phenomenon of somnambulism, a deeper trance, was discovered in the 19th century by Count Maxime de Puysegut, a student of Mesmer. The mind is completely relaxed, either by a group of instructions in the form of a suggestion or just spontaneously, as can occur in some subjects. To achieve this state by suggestion the words used are very important and need to be consistent. (The word somnambulism as used in hypnosis terms should not be confused with its dictionary definition, which is 'sleep walking'.)

Stage hypnotists rely on this depth of hypnosis, as the subjects can still talk, open their eyes and carry out tasks. It is also called 'waking' hypnosis. A popular demonstration to prove the phenomenon of trance is to ask a hypnotized subject to pick a number between 1 and 10, then instruct him to eliminate the chosen number from his memory and to forget the instruction also. The subconscious will do this as it holds no threat to the person involved.

The suggestions given when the subject is in somnambulism show how the mind can follow outside influence, which in this case causes partial amnesia. When the subject is asked to open his eyes, he is then instructed to count his fingers. Invariably, he misses out the number he has been asked to forget and end up with one finger spare. The subject then looks totally bemused, not knowing how he has managed to miscalculate.

## 3. The 'Coma' Trance

The coma state is a much deeper state of hypnosis. It is the only state in which the subject is catatonic, which means you can move the subject's limbs in any position, however uncomfortable it may look, and they will stay there until you move them again. The limbs feel waxy and more pliable. The subject experiences lethargy and is completely and wonderfully relaxed, his or her whole body being fully anaesthetized.

The coma state, unless used in painless surgery, is of little use for advanced forms of hypnotherapy because the subject will not respond to physical suggestions or be able to answer questions. To the stage hypnotist it is a menace. Because it is such a marvellous state for the subjects, they simply do not want to be disturbed. Before it was discovered how to terminate this trance the hypnotist would try and get the subject off the stage as soon as possible, usually failing to arouse the person, which would upset and worry the audience.

Although very rare and most unlikely, it has been known for subjects to go directly into the coma state immediately they are hypnotized. This is how the fear that a person could be 'stuck' in hypnosis originated. If left alone, these subject will bring themselves out of the trance, just as they would if they were day-dreaming. It is no more harmful than that. The most successful suggestion to terminate this type of trance is to say: 'If you do not come out of hypnosis you will never be able to go into hypnosis again.' Because it is such a pleasant state, this comment invariably brings the subject out of hypnosis.

The 'coma' state is by far the most fascinating phenomenon in hypnotism, the dread of ancient times and the cause of a great deal of the fear surrounding hypnosis. Yet it is highly likely that, if you wanted to experiment with this phenomenon, you would not be lucky enough to find someone who would go spontaneously into this condition.

## *A Guide for Guides*

Practice and confidence are necessary for you to guide a subject through the preliminary stages of trance. The subject needs to be reassured that you know what you are doing, so he can relax. If you start to giggle out of embarrassment, then you will lose the confidence of your subject and it will take some time to regain it sufficiently for him to be in a position to relax adequately in order for you to guide him into a deep trance.

Other things that will hinder your subject are stuttering, tripping over your words or, even worse, to keep apologizing for whatever you are doing that is incorrect. This will certainly lose credibility with your subject. Because the belief system of your subject is important to overcoming resistance, the above scripts should be read and taken seriously.

Unfortunately, in the Western world we do not have the respect for the power of the mind that people have in the East. They have been brought up with the knowledge of the power of the mind and so find it easier to accept.

Imagine that you had to go into a business meeting with a managing director to sell a product and the product was a mediocre one, no different to many others on the market. The executive's acceptance of it would be based on your selling ability rather than on the product itself. In order to have an edge on your competition you would have to generate absolute confidence in your approach. Just one stammer in your very important sales pitch could spoil any chances you may have had to make a sale.

Inducing hypnosis is similar in the fact that subjects need to feel comfortable. Although you can regain their confidence much more easily than if you were trying to make a sale, because they have come to you for help you need to understand the importance of the induction and suggestions and how vital it is that you put them over successfully. To help you over this preliminary hurdle you should practise by yourself, reading the inductions and suggestions thoroughly, carefully and repeatedly. Familiarize yourself with them completely.

Even better is to record yourself and listen to this tape until you are satisfied your words flow smoothly and with strength. You do not need to memorize the words. You can easily read them, although you should attempt to disguise the fact you are reading. Say the words as if you were in conversation to generate interest. Emphasize the words that will have an impact for the subject's particular problem.

## How to Induce Hypnotic 'Coma'

It is important that each step is completed successfully before going to the next stage. When all the stages have been achieved, your subject should be in the 'coma' state. Note that the subject will be aware of everything that is going on. Because he may choose not to react this does not mean he has not heard you. It is very difficult to fall asleep in hypnosis. Presume your subject is awake.

### Step 1
Relax the subject into light trance by using the progressive induction.

## Step 2

Relax to the somnambulism depth of trance. A technique known as 'Losing the numbers' has been the most popular through the years. Although quite old it is a tried and trusted method for achieving somnambulism.

## Losing the Numbers

When you have achieved a pleasant, deep relaxation, continue with the induction into somnambulism. An example is given below:

> 'Good.....now you have relaxed your body.....so deeply relaxed.....I know you will want to relax your mind.....and it's very simple to relax your mind.....I'm going to show you how.....in a moment.....I am going to ask you to count aloud backwards from 100.....each time you say a number, I want you to see it in your mind.....and between each number you will say the words "deeper and deeper".....and each time you say the words "deeper and deeper", the number relaxes away.....and as the number disappears to allow the next number to appear, you go five times deeper into relaxation.....so you will find that by the time you reach about 95.....you will be so relaxed that all the numbers will just have disappeared.....there will be no more numbers.....good.....when you cannot find the next number, you just say "gone".....when you can't find the numbers you will feel so marvellous.....when you're ready, first picture the number in your mind's eye before you say it.....so let's begin.'

The subject will proceed to count down from 100. Encourage him to say "deeper and deeper" by first saying the words yourself, with him. As he is following your instructions, you talk over his words very quietly, but so he can hear, and even purposely distract him, gently and soothingly, with your own soothing encouragement. You say: 'As you say each number your mind relaxes so much so that the numbers in your mind seem to drift further and further away.'

If the subject is just carrying on with the numbers without faltering, he cannot be following the instructions properly and you are not getting his full co-operation. If this is the case, count him out of hypnosis and explain this, then start again. Try a fantasy trip or deep relaxation script, if you think it will help. Otherwise, continue...

> '*And you feel yourself drifting deeper and deeper.....and that's fine.....and the next one.....the numbers are getting smaller and fainter now.....getting so small and faint as you drift deeper and deeper.....nearly all gone now.....*'

When the subject tells you the numbers have disappeared, say to him: 'How does it feel? Feels good, doesn't it?'

The theory behind 'Losing the numbers' is that the suggestion is causing distraction and overloading the brain with complicated and difficult instructions that, on the surface, seem to the subject easy. This causes the mind to 'crash' like a computer that has been overloaded. This just means that the subject's conscious takes a back seat and the subconscious comes forward and takes the instructions literally.

Each time, the subconscious follows a set of instructions that has a cause and effect, for example, 'If you do this, that will happen.' When this is proven to the subconscious it will follow more readily and quickly. That is why when someone has been in hypnosis before each proceeding time becomes easier and quicker for him. Self-hypnosis, when practised daily, can be tuned so finely that the subject can use a trigger thought which can immediately put him in deep trance even with his eyes open.

Few people go into true somnambulism without passing through artificial somnambulism. In order to go from the light trance to the deep trance with Losing the numbers, they go through this artificial state in which the numbers are still remembered but there is an unwillingness to say them aloud. That is why it is important to ask the subject if the numbers have now gone.

## Step 3

Explain to the subject that there is a basement of trance and that in order for him to reach this wonderful deep relaxation you will be deepening his hypnosis by certain exercises for the mind. To take the subject to the bottom floor of trance, you double his present state of hypnosis (after reaching somnambulism) three times. It is important that each stage is followed precisely. The following is one of the methods for reaching deep trance.

Explain to the subject while they are in hypnosis that there is an even deeper state of relaxation than they are already experiencing—the bottom floor of hypnosis:

> 'If you want, I will help you reach it. To reach this level you must go down three more floors. We are going to call the floors A, B and C. To reach the first floor, you must double the relaxation you already have. To get down to floor B you have to relax twice as much again as you did at floor A and when you get down to floor C, you have reached the basement of relaxation. At that point you will show signs by which I will be able to tell that you are at your basement

*of relaxation. You don't know what these signs are and I don't need to tell you, but every person who has ever been at the basement of relaxation gives off these signs.*

*'So let's begin. I want you now to double your relaxation and when you reach floor A say "A".....[wait until the subject says the letter "A"]. When you reach floor B you will find it difficult to pronounce the letter "B", but try your utmost to say it aloud. [Some subjects will fail to say "B". This is an excellent sign. When you feel reasonably sure they have reached floor B, continue]. We are now going to floor C. In order to reach floor C, just double your relaxation. You might find it too difficult to move your lips sufficiently to say "C", but try.'*

When you are sure the subject has reached floor C, you need to test for anaesthesia at this point before you continue. The hypnotherapist may use an Alice or towel clamp (such as a dentist would use) and test for anaesthesia. Pricking the subject with needles is not recommended because of the possibility of infection. If you pinch the skin at the top of the subject's hand and twist it, that should give you some indication. Without any further suggestion from you, the subject should not experience any discomfort.

If the subject needs extra suggestions, you have not achieved the 'coma' state. If the subject has achieved complete anaesthesia, he is ready for the next test.

## Step 4
Ask your subject to try to lift a leg (or to move any other group of muscles). There may be some slight movement in the upper area of the leg, but if he is unable to move or lift it he is ready for the next test.

## Step 5

Ask the subject to open his eyes. Do not suggest they will not open. Just say: 'Try to open your eyes'. If the eyes open or if you notice even a slight movement under the eye lids, then take the subject down another flight and double the relaxation. With a true coma state, the tiny eye muscles will not move at all. Only when this test has been successful should you try the next test.

## Step 6

The next test is for catatonia. Stretch the subject's arm out to the side or in front. If the catatonic state exists, the arm will remain in the position it was placed. This should again be accomplished without any verbal suggestions. When you extend the arm, hold it for a couple of seconds and then gradually lessen your support. If the arm begins to drop, increase your support and give a slight tug or move the arm or hand in a certain position to indicate it should remain that way.

It is important that each test is successfully completed before proceeding to the next one. When all tests have been completed in the above order, you can be sure the subject is in the 'coma' state. Remember, your subject will not be able to react to physical suggestions but can hear and understand everything at all times. If physical control of movement is necessary, the subject will have to be brought up to a lighter level of trance and returned to the bottom level when finished.

## *Terminating the 'Coma' State*

Because subjects enjoy a state of euphoria while in the 'coma' state, it is often difficult to bring them out of it. For this reason, the following seems to be the most effective method:

'If you want to enjoy this state of relaxation again, you will open your eyes at the count of one; otherwise, you will never be able to achieve this state again.'

Perseverance will achieve such a state but you also have to have the co-operation of your subjects. If their belief structure is such that they have no confidence in you because it is your first attempt at hypnotizing them, this could be a barrier. With a hypnotherapist, clients have complete faith and will follow instructions without too much criticism.

# four

# USING SELF-HYPNOSIS TO BETTER YOUR LIFE

In Chapter 3 you learned how to put yourself into hypnosis, either alone or with the help of a volunteer to guide you. Now we are going to take things a stage further. What happens once you are in hypnosis and are deeply relaxed, your subconscious ready to receive the new programme you want to implant into your mind to achieve the change in behaviour that you desire?

In this chapter you will find a number of post-hypnotic suggestions, each one in the form of a script that you can use to help you address whatever problem is troubling you, or to help you to bring about the enhancement and improvement in your life that you hope for. All you need to do is record the script yourself onto a tape recorder, or ask your 'home therapy helper' to read the suggestion to you once you are in hypnosis.

The construction of a suggestion is extremely important. It would be a pity if your treatment were to fail, leaving you believing that advanced therapy was necessary when really it was just the composition of the suggestion that was at fault. There are certain rules applicable in compiling your suggestion but they are by no means hard and fast. For example, the stop smoking suggestion I have been using for years is full of negative words—generally a no-no in hypnosis circles—but it has proved extremely successful for me and my clients.

When dealing with the mind there are many variables; what works for one person may not work for another. However, the rules listed below are a good general guide to designing your own individual script. The rules I have chosen are important in formulating a powerful suggestion. If you try them and are still not getting a result, then you should consider seeking the services of an advanced hypnotherapist (see Useful Addresses, page 177).

## DEVELOPING YOUR OWN SCRIPT

The options for self-hypnosis were covered in Chapter 3. If you choose to undertake hypnosis without a helper, then be sure to read through the rules below. You can either use your own script or use the ones provided. Feel free to personalize these to suit your own needs.

When you have chosen your script, then put it on a cassette tape and play it back. Practise it until you are satisfied that your voice is soothing and even. Begin the tape with a few moments of silence. This is to allow you time to get from the tape machine to wherever you are going to relax and to have time to compose yourself.

Make sure you are comfortable, either seated or lying down. Uncross your legs, let your arms fall naturally at your sides and make sure your neck is supported. Your tape should begin with the progressive relaxation (see pages 57–60) and be followed by the appropriate suggestion, then end with counting out of hypnosis (see page 70). Grammatically, you can use either the first or second person on the tape, that is: 'I feel more confident...' or 'You feel more confident...'

When you are reading the progressive induction, use a slow, monotonous type of voice, while the suggestion should be more enthusiastic and businesslike. The count out of hypnosis, on the other hand, should be done in a strong and forceful voice, still holding the enthusiasm.

## HYPNOTIZING YOURSELF WITHOUT THE AID OF A TAPE RECORDER

This is not easy, I have to admit. Most people have access to a tape recorder these days but not everyone has the necessary equipment. Also, some people may suffer from technophobia, a fear of technology. So for the person who does not want to or who cannot use a tape recorder, then I am afraid you will have to try and memorize the progressive script as completely as you can. Ideally this is a classic situation in which you would be best off enlisting the aid of someone to help guide you into hypnosis by reading the induction and suggestion to you. Either that or perhaps you can persuade a friend to make a tape for you, lend you his or her machine and switch it on for you before leaving.

Before you start with the hypnosis, prepare your script and read it aloud a couple of times. Pick a word that signifies what change you want; for example, if you want to sleep more soundly, you could choose the word 'slumber'. This becomes your *trigger* word; you will be using it to programme your subconscious.

When you have relaxed yourself, either by a tape

recording or just mentally going through the progressive relaxation in your mind's eye, then, at the point you have finished your induction, just instruct your subconscious to come forward in the form of a picture or thought. Whatever comes forward in your mind, even if it is a blank, say your key word, for example 'slumber'. This will programme your subconscious for change. Your mind will have accepted the scripted suggestion in your short-term memory when you read the script aloud, as mentioned above.

The word 'slumber,' in this case, just acts as a trigger word. It is like pressing the enter key on a computer which activates the programme. The two major obstacles to prevent the work going ahead would be either if you have not attained hypnosis or if the problem were linked with an early trauma. If the latter, this trauma would have to be dealt with before the new programme could be put into action (see the client case histories dealing with sleep problems in Chapter 5). However, repetition of the appropriate suggestion may in time eliminate the trauma block.

There are countless different and varied induction and suggestion scripts to put yourself into self-hypnosis when working alone. Below are some golden rules for writing your own. There is no reason why, by carefully following the suggested scripts, you cannot achieve a good, deep hypnosis by yourself. However, I still recommend having a helper, if at all possible, to guide you into hypnosis on your first venture. Once you have experienced it then you should feel confident enough on future occasions to be able to hypnotize yourself.

## 10 Rules for Formulating a Suggestion

1. Use the Present Tense
2. Be Positive
3. Be Specific
4. Be Detailed
5. Keep it Simple
6. Use Exciting, Imaginative Words
7. Be Realistic
8. Be Personalized
9. Symbolize Your Suggestion
10. Be Repetitive

Now let us look at these rules in more detail...

### Use the Present Tense

Always suggest that you are already acting out the behaviour change you desire. Say 'I am confident' or 'I have confidence', for example.

The only exception to this rule is if you are presently suffering from a physical condition, such as a broken leg. In this case use a progressive form of the present tense: 'My leg heals quickly and comfortably.' Or you can suggest to yourself: 'My leg heals in half the time it would normally take,' in order to lock in a time element. Direct suggestions for future behaviour must also be in the present tense: 'I always feel comfortable in company,' 'Day by day, I feel more enthusiastic about...' or 'I am more sure of myself.'

## Be Positive

Eliminate negative words and phrases such as 'I am not...' or 'I do not...' Create a mental picture of what you want to move towards as if it has already happened: 'I am more confident,' *not* 'I will be more confident,' or 'I would like to feel more confident.'

## Be Specific

Confine your suggestions to one area and do not try to cover a collection of problems all at once. For example, do not tell yourself: 'I feel confident, I control my weight and I sleep soundly.' This is like the lazy man and his load—he tries to carry far too much so that he will not have to make a return journey, and he ends up dropping everything he is carrying and making more work for himself. So, do not overload your subconscious with a selection of major problems.

## Be Detailed

Analyse your goal and structure your script to cover every detail of your changed behaviour attitude. Do not just say you want to succeed but detail in what way, which goals you would like to reach. For example, you might specify precisely how much money you wish to earn or what size business you require for you to attain your goal in life. Otherwise, the subconscious—which tends to take things literally—may just believe that keeping a roof over your head and food in the larder is your idea of being successful because you have neglected to explain just how successful you want to be.

Do not forget that your ideas of success are changing constantly as you mature and progress. You do not want your subconscious to act on out-of-date information; therefore you reprogramme it using your imagination and visualization.

Consciously, you may want riches. Your subconscious, on the other hand, may still be acting under the impression that just having a job (any job) is enough, as this was once perhaps your idea of complete success. Thus your subconscious may believe its instructions have already been carried out and that no further work is necessary. Have you ever wondered why some people stay in a job they loathe, year after year, for all of their working lives? Now you know why—because they have failed to reprogramme their subconscious *in detail* as to what they really want to achieve.

Suggest the *exact* improvement you wish to achieve. It is of little use saying: 'I would like to be...' or 'I will feel better when...' The word 'will' suggests a future action and could be misconstrued by the subconscious as meaning some point in the distant future. This request has been diluted, so it gives the subconscious a get-out. It could be requesting a change in 10 years—no time-frame has been locked into the suggestion.

## Keep it Simple

Speak to your subconscious as if you were talking to a toddler. The subconscious may well be very sophisticated but there is less chance of confusion if you keep the wording plain. The English language is full of words that have innuendoes and double meanings, so think carefully before you give your orders to your subconscious.

I knew an American hypnotherapist who for years wanted to give up smoking. She was also permanently worried about her weight. In hypnosis she instructed her subconscious to replace the satisfaction she felt smoking with becoming thin. Her use of the word 'thin' turned out to be the problem. 'Thin' in her conscious mind meant slim, but her subconscious took the word literally. She became painfully thin, just as she had instructed. She looked dreadful but, like the anorexic, she thought she looked slim.

Also, this self-inflicted programme included an extensive fitness campaign to make sure no weight was put on. It was more a fitness compulsion; she was running a few miles a day to ensure she kept 'thin' and she would keep up the regime, however impractical, even to the extent of having to go out running in the tea-break of a conference when everyone else was socializing. This is a perfect example of a communication breakdown between the conscious and the subconscious.

## Use Exciting, Imaginative Words

The subconscious reacts to emotive words. Make your suggestions full of feeling and excitement. Old-fashioned words often have impact. They may have been used in fairy stories or comic books and, even though buried deep in your subconscious files, when located they are still powerful words.

*Exciting. Wonderful. Dynamic.* Words like these, to the subconscious, will be acted on their true meanings and encourage the desired change. Although the words may seem uncomfortable to the acting home therapist, and be words you may not generally use, to the person in hypnosis they are very soothing, comfortable and encourage enthusiasm.

Also, some people may feel happier with flowery words, describing in detail the wonders of surrounding scenery, etc., while another may find this uninteresting and boring. Therefore, I have included two different approaches to suggestions in the examples below.

## Be Realistic

There are circumstances in which it is wrong to suggest perfection. For example, saying 'I am happy all the time' would not be a realistic suggestion—suppose you then had to go to a funeral!

## Be Personalized

Structure your suggestions for the change you want in yourself, your attitudes and actions. As you change, others around you will change as well. The easiest way to initiate change in the people around you is to change yourself. If you are in a relationship that is suffering from constant arguments and you stop responding to negativity from your partner, he or she, too, will have to change and either find a new way of aggravating you or give up arguing completely. Whatever the outcome there will be a change in your partner's strategy. Therefore, you can programme yourself to react totally indifferently to a word or phrase that normally would stimulate your anger.

For example: 'Each time my partner/friend/someone

says [offending words].....I feel relaxed and calm, knowing that I am now in control of my emotions. My subconscious deals with any negative emotions, constructively channelling them to my advantage, allowing me to be relaxed and calm.' It may be appropriate to have an anger-release suggestion prior to this suggestion. If you have a locked-in anger about a person or circumstance, it can cause deep anxiety and rage and even affect your health. A good anger-release suggestion can dissipate the unwanted reactions (see page 120).

## Symbolize Your Suggestion

Picture yourself as you want to be. Build a detailed image in your imagination. Do not worry if it is exaggerated, as long as there is at least a small possibility of its coming true. That gives you a gigantic scope, as most dreams are possible if you are willing to work at them.

When I lived in California in the early 1980s, I was told that the US government would never clamp down on drink-driving as the liquor barons had too much money involved in politics.

One mother had both her children killed by drunken drivers so she channelled all her anger and disgust into getting justice and preventing it happening to others. She put her full energy into changing the law. She was just an ordinary housewife but she persevered against all the odds and was quickly joined by other mothers. They picketed, found a slogan that attracted TV coverage—MADD (Mothers Against Drunk Drivers)—and changed history in only a short time after a brave campaign. Now the drink-driving laws in the US are stricter than they are in the UK. Virtually anything is possible if you hold fast to a dream.

## Be Repetitive

Use repetition but with varied synonymous words and convincing adjectives, so your suggestion is attractive. It is a little like selling a product. The more often you picture an idea the more of a possibility it becomes.

For example, when you see fashions such as the mini-skirt, platform heels and bell-bottoms, you may think they look very outdated these days. But when you are exposed to the same fashions by media coverage and constantly told that this is now the latest in fashion trends, you start to become accustomed to the old/new look. The more you see it, the less outmoded it seems. In the same way, you can bombard your subconscious with propaganda until it believes it!

With these guides to suggestion in mind, you can either use one of the structured scripts included later in this chapter as it stands or change it to suit your individual needs. You may even decide to design a whole new suggestion yourself.

If you wanted to design scripts for other people, you would need to find out exactly what changes they are expecting in their lives and behaviour and work the information around one of the basic scripts. If they wanted to play a sport better, for example, you would need to know all about which skills the individual would need to develop in order to play the chosen game well. For example, in tennis a problem for many players is that they tend to take their eyes off the ball just before they hit it. A new habit needs to be created, so you might put this instruction into the suggestion: 'Your eyes stay fixed on the ball until your racket strikes it, which enables you to direct the ball exactly where you want it to go. Your co-ordination is perfect, your arm movements strong and positive.'

Generally, it is accepted that the script for suggestions has to be long and repetitive. Having said this, I myself discovered quite by accident that this was not always necessary. When I developed the speed reading script that I use with clients I found that a short, direct instruction was all that was needed. Which is all well and good when you are an experienced therapist, knowing your skill and having already gained the subject's confidence. But for the amateur without the benefit of experience, the long, descriptive script generates the kind of trust and confidence in hypnosis you need.

I like to reassure subjects before they go into hypnosis that they can reject any suggestions that are inappropriate. This tends to dispel any worries subjects may still be harbouring about being 'brainwashed'. I use the following short, comforting script to help to prepare the subconscious, after the progressive relaxation but before the suggestion.

## INTRODUCTION PRIOR TO THE SUGGESTION

*'In this deep and special sleep.....your subconscious mind.....for your safekeeping.....monitors everything that is happening around you.....Therefore, these suggestions, because they are for your benefit, go directly to your*

*subconscious mind.....where they are accepted. These
thoughts become established.....firmly fixed.....deeply.....in
your inner system.....embedded, so these suggestions remain
with you.....long after you open your eyes. These new
thoughts help you to begin to change the things you want
to change.....these changes allow you to enjoy your life more
and more, day by day.'*

# A QUALITY-OF-LIFE PLAN
# FOR A BETTER FUTURE

When you have succeeded in hypnotizing yourself regularly,
a quick, daily input into your subconscious of three impact
words, which literally takes seconds, will start to activate
your wanted changes without the need for lengthy hypnosis
sessions.

You must first find three powerful words that epitomize
the changes you want. Words such as *exciting*, *successful*,
*dynamic*, *forceful*, *charismatic* and *confident*, for example.
Choose the three words that you feel best conjure up your
wishes and ambitions.

When you have put yourself in hypnosis, access your
subconscious by instructing it to come forward in the
form of a picture or a thought. You can use the same
picture or thought each time, if you feel comfortable with
it, or wait for one to come at random. Say your three
chosen words privately in your mind and, as you say
them, picture yourself on a TV screen behaving in the
way you would like to see yourself in a real situation.
Then open your eyes.

Do this every day for at least three weeks and you will start to see changes in your attitudes. It is a simple blueprint for improvement.

## LET'S TALK ABOUT STRESS

### *Stress Relief*

Stress is one of the greatest problems in our materialistic and possession-conscious society and the magician who can promise prompt relief from it will be much sought after. With stress management courses popping up all over the place, stress relief programmes will be the treatment of the future and any cash used to develop ways of preventing stress before it causes illness will be money well spent. Hypnosis, the quickest and most natural relaxing power we have at our fingertips, has a vital role to play. It can calm and rest the mind in seconds. Meditation is the next best method, its only disadvantage being the time it takes. Hypnosis is the key to obtaining deep relaxation in a fraction of the time it would normally take with standard meditation practice.

We rarely leave time for this all important repose. In ancient days, before doing battle at sunrise an army would retire to be pampered, massaged, oiled and wrapped in towels, to rest and calm the mind to prepare for war and perhaps death. In the 1990s we have pressure at work and pressure at home and little, if any, time for calming ourselves. The best we seem able to achieve as a form of relaxation is either drinking alcohol excessively or watching TV. We even use gruelling, body-sapping exercise as a form of relieving anxiety. We live in such an uptight, pressure-filled society and yet, still, hypnosis is forced to take a back seat as it has so often done.

We fight to keep our houses, cars and valuables. When the recession of the 1980s struck, many had to accept that their property had suddenly been devalued, fortunes were lost overnight and many people realized that, in fact, they did not own anything at all. We have been programmed to surround ourselves with valuables and strive to get what we have not already yet attained.

The structure of family life has also changed, making it often impossible to live near grandparents, parents or other relatives as was once the norm. A generation of children are growing up with little hope of a job. Small wonder that we are acquiring stress-related illnesses and that violence and aggression are on the increase.

Technology and sophisticated equipment have played their part in causing thousands upon thousands of redundancies. Those people still left with a job are under immense pressure simply to keep it. Apart from these new pressures forced on our society, we have had to adjust to a slow build-up of stress through the centuries, mostly due to our supposedly becoming more 'civilized'.

### Peace in Paradise?

Many books talk about stress and what life used to be like without it. I can claim first-hand knowledge. I found a small paradise island where stress was unknown. The island was self-sufficient and had the comfort of all-year-round warmth. It was not subjected to tornadoes, earthquakes or tidal waves, as so many other islands are. I watched as within just under two years this island, situated in the Far East, became what I now call the Billion Dollar Island. The government decided to promote it, made it tax-free and suddenly the people who owned the beach-front properties became multi-millionaires.

When I first visited it it had no entertainment and the islanders were what we would call 'uncivilized'. I visited it a few times and then decided to make it my home for part of every year. I would be away for a few months and each time I returned, the island would have changed. Thirty-six hotels were constructed within a year. A hundred million dollars was spent on one road through the jungle. In spite of all this upheaval there was a group of people living there who did not suffer from stress at all. They did not know what it was.

While all this construction was going on, these islanders kept to themselves, just taking life slowly as they had always done. All the workers for the five-star hotels had to be flown in from the mainland. The fact was that the islanders did not need to work in these new enterprises because they did not have any compulsion for material things. I mistakenly thought that these new marvels around them would entice them. They did not. The weather is hot all year round and even the rainy season is warm. Food grows plentifully and the sea is full of fish.

I could not quite understand why the islanders remained unaffected by all the wealth around them. But I started to understand when a wise old man from the mainland told me a story. It went like this:

*A businessman was chatting to an islander who had just caught a fish. 'How many fish do you catch?' the businessman inquired.*

*'Just one,' replied the fisherman.*

*'How many do you normally catch?' asked the businessman.*

*'I only eat one a day, so I only catch one a day,' said the fisherman.*

*'If you caught two a day you could eat one and sell one,' the businessman suggested.*

*'Why?' the fisherman asked.*

*'Well,' the businessman continued, 'if you sell an extra fish a day you can save enough to buy a boat.'*

*'Why?' repeated the fisherman.*

*'When you buy your boat, you can save up to buy another boat.'*

*'Why?' questioned the fisherman.*

*'With the extra money you can buy a fleet of boats.'*

*'Why?' the fisherman asked patiently.*

*'Well,' said the businessman triumphantly, 'if you have a fleet of boats, soon you will be have enough money to retire to a paradise island!'*

When I was living on this wonderful island I knew exactly how the islander felt. I was organizing hypnotherapy courses in Malaysia and I suddenly thought to myself, 'Why? I could live here permanently, without all the hassle of work, stress and worry. Just write my book and relax.' Then it dawned on me that all of the paradise spots in the world I had visited had this one disadvantage: the so-called civilized person quickly gets bored, not being used to the slower pace of life.

The major problem for the outsider who decides to settle in these idyllic havens, surrounded by beauty, is alcoholism. I sat in the new beach bars and watched the new inhabitants drink themselves into a stupor. That was the extent of their 'new-found' life. So there is not always peace in paradise. Paradise, as I have mentioned before, is all in the mind.

## What Is Stress?

Before we can treat stress, we should know a little about it. Stress is the reaction of the autonomic nervous system in defending itself against attack, real or imagined. The nervous system's original design was to protect us from physical threats. The system releases adrenalin to assist in the 'fight or flight' response. Once the threat subsides, the system returns to normal because the adrenalin has been used up either fighting or running away. If the adrenalin remains unused, however, and remains in the system, the result is what we know of as stress.

Major stresses of our modern world include the death of a spouse, close relative or friend, divorce or a change in marital lifestyle, redundancy, moving house, illness, work pressure, financial problems and the inability to achieve one's goals.

Then there are the daily, minor stresses which we all know, too numerous to list individually. Modern food production creates stress, especially if we eat the meat of animals who knew they were going to die. These animals release adrenalin into their bloodstream, which is then added to our own. Greed also causes stress, as does pride.

The cause of stress may remain locked in the subconscious for long periods of time. This is where hypnosis can be extremely useful, as it can help us to re-evaluate past stressful experiences. For example, a woman who loses a child at birth will still be affected long after the event. Some painful events in childhood can linger a whole lifetime. It is even suggested by those who believe in reincarnation that past life traumas can be responsible for stress problems. Merely being a human being is stressful!

Since stress is adrenalin-based, all stress weakens the nervous system because energy from non-essential organs is being drained to support the adrenalin flow. At the first sign of an aggressor (or what the emotions perceive as one) the nervous system automatically channels non-essential energy to the organs of action. When confronted by a tiger at 12 paces, the last thing one wants to do is have an intellectual debate with oneself about whether to go to the left or right. So the system automatically bypasses the intellect and reacts instantaneously.

When there is an excess of adrenaline thinking clearly becomes impossible. The system also works at a faster rate. Eating is not required when adrenalin is flowing, so the body becomes further weakened by irregular diet. For some reason the body craves caffeine and chocolate—many stress sufferers live on these substances.

Stress weakens us, makes us less effective and, most important, isolates us from our fellow human beings. The biggest stress of all is loneliness, which is in part caused by stress, so we have a big, vicious circle.

Most of all, stress stops the experience of joy. The nervous system is thrown into a purely survival-orientated mode, and this is no fun at all. And we need fun in our lives!

Security has to be re-established before joy can be re-experienced. Since the cause of stress lies within the nervous system, it is there that all action must take place. Many stresses are purely imagined. For example, a man may feel threatened by the loss of a deal or by a woman turning him down, whereas neither occurrence is life-threatening.

If you are feeling stressed, or if you want to help someone experiencing extreme stress, the following rules can help bring reassurance before relaxation and suggestion therapy.

1. Stress is not your fault—it is a reaction of the automatic nervous system and not in the control of the voluntary system. (This can help remove any sense of guilt associated with feeling stressed.)
2. However bad, nothing is the end of the world except your death—nothing else is.
3. Eat well, sleep well, make love well, if circumstances allow.
4. Work in short, regular periods and take breaks, allowing for periods of activity and periods of rest.
5. Keep your mind occupied with varied activities.
6. Take regular relaxation. This can be taught with hypnosis.
7. Aim to earn enough money not to have to travel on public transport! (Actually, this is one of my little jokes I like to tell my students and clients. You can allow yourself the odd joke now and then—humour is one of the best weapons in combatting stress.)

## How Stress Affects the Individual Personality

An eminent Californian cardiologist and member of one of the world's leading heart research teams, Dr Ray Roseman, conducted along with his colleague Meyer Friedman a famous investigation into which type of person was most likely to have a coronary. They created a profile of a typical candidate for a heart attack, known as type 'A'. This type of personality exhibited a habitual sense of time urgency and an excessive competitive drive.

A control group of men who did not show this sense of urgency and competitive drive was then established as type 'B'. Results showed that type 'A' was found to have seven times more coronary heart disease than type 'B,' even though their lifestyles were similar.

What type of personality are you? The manner in which a person handles a situation is influenced by his or her disposition—in other words frame of mind or temperament. When you are under a lot of pressure you may remain calm or become extremely tense; it is your disposition that will determine your stress level. A very active person can thrive on high pressure levels, whereas the worrier will prefer the lower pressure levels.

Once you can identify your own or another's disposition you begin to understand the different stress levels and your vulnerability to the negative effects of stress.

Ambitious people can often push themselves too hard, whereas the more relaxed person can often be ambitious, still push, yet be much less vulnerable to the effects of pressure. Managers or personnel with senior positions always fall into one of the two categories I mentioned earlier. Type 'A' is time-driven, ambitious, competitive and prone to heart attacks.

Type 'B' is casual, less ambitious and more relaxed about time. Below I have listed five personality types you might recognize.

## Ambitious and Driven

This type of person has a strong desire for success or achievement. He is successful and driven by the ever-present need to succeed. He is highly committed to his career, extremely energetic and overactive and rarely finds time to relax. He hates to wait for anything and anyone, is extremely impatient and cannot bear to waste time. He is the classic type 'A'.

'A' types are common in senior corporate positions, since the very post requires an energetic, ambitious person to achieve the results required. He can be both aggressive and argumentative when relating to others and he has a strong need to dominate. Underneath this he often has many hidden insecurities. His home and relationships are secondary to his work commitment and, if he does go on holiday, he will invariably take his work with him, calling the office frequently and still not relaxing.

He sets himself high standards, sometimes impossibly high, but he is still driven to achieve them, as failure to do so would be too difficult to accept. He adds to his stress by overloading himself with work and working to strict, self-imposed deadlines.

He suffers with insomnia, high blood-pressure, constant restlessness and heart problems. He is usually both a heavy smoker and drinker. Although his preferred stress level is high, so is his vulnerability to the effects of stress.

## Calm and Collected

The classic calm personality does not become easily disturbed, excited or agitated. She is tranquil, even placid. She does not set impossible objectives for herself. She is both unworried and patient. She takes the time to reflect and think over her achievements. She will achieve less than the ambitious personality, but she does not become obsessed with competing with other people. She has the capacity to appreciate other people's good characteristics and to put up with other people's inadequacies. Her self-esteem is strong and she does not need to be domineering. She is seldom irritated by others and both gives and receives affection and praise easily.

She keeps the perfect balance between work and home, and takes time for her leisure pursuits. Her inner tensions are low, her stress level is medium to low and her vulnerability to the effects of stress is low.

## Conscientious and Controlled

This type of person is meticulous and takes extreme care over everything required of him. He is reliable, single minded and can often be stubborn. He can become over-obsessive in his desire to do things thoroughly and often becomes over-concerned with doing things right. He runs the risk of losing sight of long-term objectives in his pursuit of the small details. Because of his quest to do things correctly, he prefers a set routine. He can be thrown off balance by the unexpected and cannot cope with change as well as the ambitious or calm person.

He works within his own range of competence, in which he finds his security, and does not like to seek challenges in his life. He is traditional, respects authority and thereby gives respect to his superiors and expects it from his subordinates—this rigid code can affect his interaction with others. Generally, his home life will follow a similar pattern.

Because of his insecurity about losing control he can suffer a lot with inner tension and turmoil if faced with the prospect of an excessive workload. Colleagues who do not plan ahead may add to his stress.

His stress level is low to moderate but can be increased to very high levels at times of change.

### Shy and Unassertive

This person cannot assert herself and has great difficulty standing up for her rights. She is mainly concerned with pleasing others, usually in an effort to avoid conflict. Her fear of others' reactions causes her to shy away from situations rather than face them. She will interact with others in such a way that they will end up misunderstanding her, taking advantage of her or ignoring her requests. She cannot express her own needs and has problems in her relationships because she finds it hard to say no. She is often caught up in an obsessional need to please others.

She feels resentful that others take advantage of her and this creates a lot of inner tension. Because of her inability to satisfy her own needs she becomes frustrated and feels compelled to satisfy the needs of others. Because of her inner tensions her stress level is above average and her vulnerability to the effects of stress is moderate.

## Anxious and Tense

This type of person is invariably worried and tense due to his dread of even the possibility of misfortune. He finds it hard to relax. He constantly plans for every eventuality and is obsessed with doing things right, though he usually fails. He is prone to panic and this becomes evident when things do go wrong. He spends most of his time worrying about what is going to happen rather than concentrating on what is actually happening, a habit which is not usually constructive.

He is far too concerned with other people's judgments and evaluations, therefore his self-esteem and confidence are low. This in turn affects his relationships both at work and at home. He becomes insecure and uncertain about changing environments and will react defensively rather than rise to the challenge of change.

He experiences a lot of negative emotions and internal pressure, leading to a large amount of self-doubt. Challenging work, change and uncertainty make him particularly stressful.

He suffers from tension and persistent headaches, has an inability to think straight, usually depends on tranquillizers and suffers from nervous exhaustion. His vulnerability to stress is high.

## *Encouraging Relaxation*

It is extremely important to learn to relax and incorporate relaxation into your lifestyle. Relaxing is as important as working and, in fact, enables you to work better—which is why executives can benefit so much from learning self-hypnosis skills. Just as there are types who are more prone to heart attacks, there are types who are more prone to, say, cancer. Worrying can cause both.

Perhaps you can now see how important it is to recognize different personalities in connection with hypnotherapy suggestions. An individual suggestion for someone ambitious and driven would have to be constructed differently to one for someone calm and collected, unless you are playing safe and are using the basic scripts in this book. These scripts are more general rather than being aimed at particular personality types.

It is also important to realize that if you personally are calm and patient, expecting an anxious, tense individual immediately to become the same would be unrealistic. Trying for a total change of personality for yourself or anyone else would not only be unfair and impractical but also impossible with this form of therapy. It is not that powerful. However, with perseverance and a methodical approach you should be able to see some distinct improvements.

## SUGGESTION SCRIPTS

Below are some examples of suggestions for you to choose from. Most are long and flowing but some are sharp and to the point. Choose the type you feel most comfortable with. At the end of each suggestion is a short script which is meant to encourage you to continue with the relaxation on a regular basis. It also includes words for coming out of hypnosis. In the interests of saving space and to avoid repetition, I shall give the 'coming out script' only once. Do remember, therefore, to add the 'coming out' words at the end of these scripts or any you write yourself. If you want to go to sleep after a suggestion—and sometimes the feeling of peace you have achieved will be so wonderful that you may—you can do so by just ignoring the wake-up suggestion.

Here are the words you should add to the end of your/any script:

'You *always* enjoy the pleasant, relaxed feeling of self-hypnosis.....and you have an overwhelming desire to listen to this tape each day for a week.....knowing that it is changing your attitude to how you want to feel.....to how you want to be.....you always feel completely rejuvenated and refreshed when you come out of hypnosis.....because the complete, restful relaxation causes your body to become completely normalized.....your blood-pressure is normal.....your glands are working in harmony with one another.....your body chemistry is balanced.....and you feel marvellous.

'Now just relax even more and enjoy a moment of the deep and lasting impression upon your subconscious mind.....never to be removed....this moment of silence starts now.....[Pause for a moment].....In a moment I will count from five to one.....at the count of five.....your eyes will open and you will feel refreshed and comfortable.....if you wish to carry on relaxing, you will ignore the instructions to rouse yourself and either fall asleep, if that is what you would like to do, or relax for a little while and awaken naturally. Five.....four.....three.....coming up now.....two.....one.....eyes open.'

Now here are the suggestions themselves. Please remember that *all the suggestions should be preceded by the induction script* (pages 93–4).

### Stress Relief

'As you breathe in slowly......you find that breath travelling all the way through your body, bringing a wave of relaxation that dissipates all the tension you have sensed for some time......tension that has interfered with the way you want to be......tension that has interfered with your work and enjoyment......from now on all that tension will be relaxed out of your body......as you breathe out, all that negative tension will be eased out of your body......leaving room for positive and happy thoughts......your subconscious will now find a constructive way of dealing with stress and tension......

'Not all stress is negative stress......we need a certain amount of positive stress to encourage us to attain our goals......even to perform an act as simple as getting out of bed in the morning......now all your stress will be directed towards positive action......the remainder, which is just negative stress, will be breathed out of your body and disappear......actions or words that would have normally caused tension now give you a wonderful feeling of challenge......problems becomes obstacles to get round and your subconscious finds easy routes around such obstacles......your subconscious takes the responsibility to handle all worries and problems in a positive way......leaving you free to enjoy your life......be successful at what you want to achieve......and let your body function correctly......no longer hampered by negative thoughts, your body and mind in harmony.

'All doubts are replaced by a feeling of optimism......doubts are there to encourage you to look at all of your options......to help you to take the correct decisions......not to prevent you from doing something you are capable of......now you trust your subconscious to channel stress and worries into *the correct parts of your mind.....keeping the positive thoughts and energy.....and ridding you of the unwanted and damaging negative thoughts.....while transferring the energy from these negative thoughts into constructive energy.....energy is like electricity.....it is neither good.....nor bad.....it just needs to be channelled in the correct area.....to be constructive rather than destructive.*

*'As this new formula for good health is activated, you feel better and better.....more relaxed and calm.....this in turn allows the healing forces of your body and mind to repair and replace and energize you with your natural regularity.....you now look after your body and mind and treat them with the respect they deserve.....and because of this you feel stronger and stronger to cope with everyday obstacles.....so you now enjoy life even more.*

*'In a moment I will count from five to one.....and at the count of one.....your eyes will open.....and as they do.....you will feel refreshed and happy.....five.....four.....three.....coming up now.....two.....one.....eyes open.'*

## An End to Blushing

*'Imagine that you are never to be red-faced again..... embarrassment is a thing of the past.....imagination is the language to your inner feelings.....an instruction to your inner mind.....you are now instructing your inner mind.....your subconscious.....to remove the unwanted trigger that brings forward the feeling and emotions of blushing.....blushing, as you are already aware, is because of embarrassment resulting from a lack of confidence.....it can be a response from a forgotten experience in childhood when you were unconfident.....a signal that triggered an emotion belonging in childhood.....when you were a child it was a part of growing up into an adult.....when you are an adult, you have already had experiences that have been designed to build your confidence through the learning processes of life itself.....now*

*you find that you can control your confidence.....as your*
*confidence builds, you become less embarrassed and more*
*respectful of yourself.....and your confidence grows.....*

*'This new confidence allows you to cope with obstacles in*
*your life as an adult.....as you relax even more, with each deep*
*breath a wave of calm and soothing passes through your*
*body, pushing out all the negativity and doubt.....the*
*negativity and doubt that interfere with your*
*confidence.....now as you breathe in, you breathe in all the*
*positive thoughts and energy and as you breathe out, you*
*breathe out all the negative thoughts and energy.....*
*negativity comes in many forms..... stress..... tension.....*
*anxiety..... doubt..... depression..... discomfort..... insecurity*
*of all kinds and, because you realize that embarrassment is*
*now easing into the past where it belongs, this allows*
*your confidence to grow and flourish like a tree.....you*
*can walk tall, stand proud, look people in the eye as your*
*pride and self-worth grows.'*

## FIGHTING PHOBIAS

We all have fears of some kind but some fears are irrational
and can disrupt our lives. A phobia is an irrational fear such
as a fear of flying or snakes or heights. When such a fear
causes panic attacks, then it can be classed as a phobia.

People can live with phobias without it affecting or
disrupting their lives, whereas others have phobias that cause
them constant irritation or embarrassment. If you have a fear
of flying but are never in a situation that requires you to fly,
then that phobia is unlikely to bother you. On the other hand,
if you really need to fly, perhaps because of your job, and
have to organize your life around finding other means of

transport because of that fear, then it is more sensible—and probably cheaper in the long run—to have some therapy to alleviate the fear.

Hypnosis has the highest success rate of all for conquering fears and is by far the quickest method. Advanced hypnotherapy will greatly increase your success rate but you should try the suggestion method here before looking further afield.

For any phobia you can design your own suggestion based on the rules of writing a suggestion script given earlier in this chapter. But you should also include a rehearsal. Here is an example for combatting a fear of flying:

'You find that you can relax now whenever you would like to......when you are in a situation that before may have caused you anxiety when there was no need for it......you take a deep breath and a wave of relaxation flows through your body. As you feel so calm and relaxed, you imagine you are setting off for the airport......you are surprised and happy to realize that you feel relaxed and comfortable about the journey......you imagine the trip to the airport......you arrive at the airport and check your baggage in and you feel so calm and relaxed......ready for the flight and looking forward to arriving at your destination....it is now time to go to the flight lounge......as you walk along, you casually look out of the windows and see the planes taking off and landing......some are parked ready to take on more passengers......you find the sight relaxing and as you take a deep breath, you find yourself even more calm and relaxed.

'The time goes very quickly as you await your flight call and when it is announced you are looking forward to getting onto the plane and making yourself comfortable for the flight......you feel very comfortable and relaxed as you walk

*along the corridor to board the plane and find your
seat.....you feel very calm and relaxed as you watch the flight
attendant giving you your instructions.....the plane starts to
taxi to the runway and you look out of the window and, as
you do, a wonderful feeling of calm flows through you.....as
the plane revs its engine ready for take-off, you feel
confident and the engine noises relax you even more.....as
the plane takes off and settles into flight, you feel a wave of
relaxation flow through you.....and you realize you feel
content and comfortable.....you may decide to doze or
read, have a conversation or even watch the film.....whatever
your choice is, you find you are enjoying the flight and you
take advantage of the comforts offered.*

*'The plane now begins to make its descent ready to land
and, as you take a deep breath, you relax and enjoy the
descent of the plane.....the plane lands and as you prepare
to disembark, you feel refreshed and enthusiastic.....you look
back on the flight and realize you have enjoyed the journey.'*

(There are more suggestion scripts for handling different
phobias later in this chapter.)

As I mentioned earlier, most suggestion scripts should
always emphasize positive aspects rather than negative
ones. One of the exceptions to this rule is smoking, where
it is necessary to impress on the subconscious the unpleasant
aspects of the habit one wishes to get rid of.

### Stopping Smoking

*'You have now made one of the most important decisions
of your life.....to save your life.....by giving up smoking—
giving up polluting your lungs—your lungs are the most
important functions in your body—without them you
cannot breathe—you cannot live—it is essential for you to*

keep your lungs clean and fill them with fresh air.....so you can live.....and be healthy.

'Your body has to cope with pollution from the air that you breathe.....your lungs are adaptable and can cope with this.....but the extra strain that smoking brings about.....the extra concentrated pollution you are sucking in from each cigarette.....is weakening your insides.....your mouth, your throat, your lungs, your stomach and your blood are just a few of the victims of your carelessness.....the dangerous chemicals that are used in the pesticides sprayed on the tobacco as it grows are used to kill insects.....but is slowly killing you.....you have been forcing people around you, even young children, to breathe in your extra pollution.....you have been ignorant to how unsociable it has become.....no more.....now you care about yourself and the people around you.

'From now on you will find that you are more and more conscious that smoking is bad for you.....you are more and more aware of the damage it is doing to your health.....that it is increasing by many times your chances of dying a horrible and painful death from cancer or heart disease.....you imagine yourself fighting and struggling for breath.....or suffering with severe damage to your limbs and arteries.

'You may fool yourself that this time is a long way off.....but you know it will catch up with you eventually.....you know that smoking is doing serious damage to your general level of fitness.....you are aware of a shortage of breath when you try to run for a bus or play a sport or even walk upstairs.....you hate the unpleasant taste in your mouth and throat.....you hate the way that smoke makes your hair and clothes smell, especially when you know that other people around you are noticing it, too.....so many people have been able to give up now and they notice it more when you smell of smoke.....even being *beside you makes their own clothes smell.*

'You know how much smoking is costing you and how much better you can spend the money on other things......you know that deep down you are lying to yourself when you tell yourself that smoking calms and relaxes you......you know it is really only making you more tense......it is no longer sociable, in fact the smoker is now a misfit......a danger to non-smokers forcing them to become passive smokers against their will.*

'You find the thought of a cigarette so disgusting that you do not want to even pick one up......from now on you cut off any urge to have a cigarette before it even strikes you......by relaxing and slowing down your breathing......as you do this, the urge to smoke disappears......your subconscious is finding safe ways to get rid of your smoking habit...... redirecting the satisfaction to a good habit more advantageous to you......you have no desire at all from now on to smoke......your craving has gone forever.*

'The whole idea of smoking is offensive to you......you just don't need it any more......your inner mind finds safe and effective ways to rid yourself of this revolting habit......and as your complete mastery over your former smoking habit increases, you become proud of your self-control and willpower......your lungs and throat feel so much clearer......you have much more energy......you feel so much more relaxed......even food tastes so much better and you enjoy it so much more......although you find your appetite doesn't increase, you feel more like eating healthy foods and so you find you are able to maintain your desired weight much more easily while protecting your body from the poison of further smoking......your inner mind automatically balancing your food intake to keep you fit and healthy......your resistance to illness and disease increases steadily day by day......now just take a deep breath and relax......[Pause for 30 seconds]*

This next part is in addition to the above script but forms a piece of imagery to help to change your attitudes. It is a mild form of aversion therapy.

> *'I want you to imagine yourself in an empty room, with just you sitting at a table and all around you is the collected tar from all the cigarettes you have ever smoked.....it is collected in an ugly, glutinous mass on the ceiling.....and it is dripping down.....down.....down onto your hair and running down your face....down your forehead and cheeks.....and into your eyes and your mouth.....and running down your throat.....it's revolting.....and now you find the thought of cigarettes brings this obnoxious vision into your mind.....this reminds you how harmful they are and you now can see clearly the poison that they represent to your finely balanced body.....you no longer need or want to smoke.'*

## LOSING WEIGHT (1)

With this suggestion you should lose, comfortably, three pounds a week, sometimes more on the first week. But if you are expecting to lose lots of weight very quickly, you may find yourself disappointed. The reason is that the body will have a reaction and this may end up with you bingeing and putting all the weight back on. If you have a weight problem and have been on many diets, you will be familiar with this pattern: 'Lose fast and gain fast.' When you lose weight slowly, the body balances itself out and you are less likely to regain the unwanted weight.

'Because you want to be and enjoy your desired weight.....to your pleasure you find your weight is reducing..... gradually.....safely.....and steadily. You are happy.....secure and confident in the knowledge that you eat more rationally.....eating healthier food.....you eat less.....but enjoy the food you eat more.....you discover, to your pleasure, that you are fully satisfied on smaller amounts of food.....your metabolism works at an increased speed....: burning up the small amounts of food that you enjoy eating and ensuring that your body stays firm and slim. You are thrilled with your reflection in the mirror.....you are amazed at how much healthier and more energetic you feel.....and how much more you enjoy life.....you radiate vitality and you are proud of your new healthy body.'

### The Weight Problem Script (2)

'Because you want to lose weight and become healthier and fitter, each day you eat food that you know is good for you.....you enjoy healthier food.....you no longer crave high-calorie, rich foods and enjoy eating low-calorie, healthy foods.....your subconscious knows which foods are good for you.....and allows you to lose weight at the rate suitable for your body.....day by day you eat only when you are physically hungry.....and you eat and want only those foods that are good for your body.....you always sit down when you eat and you enjoy drinking water.....you find it is cool and refreshing and you like the taste.....you find yourself much more thirsty than you formerly were.....your stomach is smaller and getting smaller with every day that passes.....you visualize your stomach being small.

'You always leave food on your plate.....you now realize that when you have had sufficient.....the food left on your plate is wasted food.....it is of no benefit for you to eat it..... it is waste. You no longer consider your stomach a waste bin.....you respect your stomach and your body.....and *you don't force unwanted food into it because of misguided feelings of guilt.....not wanting to waste food.....the food will be wasted whether you put it in your stomach or in the waste bin.....day by day you are enjoying a new eating habit.....you only think of the bite that is in your mouth.....you enjoy the taste of it much more.....your taste buds become more sensitive and you get much more satisfaction from each bite. You eat more slowly.....you eat much less.....but you enjoy it more.....you are looking better and you are feeling better.....you feel good about yourself.'*

## No More Alcohol

This is a suggestion for those who feel they may be drinking too much and who wish to give it up altogether. If you want to cut down on your alcohol intake and drink more sensibly, then you can tailor the words according to your own desires.

*'Imagine you are in a beautiful garden.....study the wildlife.....listen to the birds.....if you listen carefully you can hear them singing.....imagine them drinking the rainwater and, as they do, you realize that some alcohol has dripped into the water the birds and, perhaps, animals are drinking from.....making them ill and disturbing their natural balance.....look on the serious side, the effects this alcohol has on their finely balanced metabolism. Alcohol is from nature but it is made by man and no longer natural with all the chemicals that have been added.....it is no longer pure as in days of old.....even then it had its harmful effects, but now the body and mind have to struggle with the chemical reactions.*

'The side-effects are the heavy hangovers you never used to get.....feeling ill or not quite right.....you know it's because of the alcohol.....looking as if you can't hold your drink.....which is true or you wouldn't want to change.....but you do want to change.....you want to feel healthy and strong and confident.....confident you are always in control of yourself and the circumstances around you. The confidence you derived from drinking alcohol is now natural to you..... you have the added confidence without the necessity to drink alcohol.

'Alcohol has shown you that you have the confidence..... now you no longer need the alcohol.....imagine now that you are going to throw away all the alcohol down the drain..... watch yourself pouring the alcohol away.....even your once favourite is now discarded.....You no longer want it.....you have been killing yourself with alcohol.....you want your body to look after you and you want to look after your body, respect it and not to abuse it.

'To you, the alcohol is a poison.....all alcohol can give you is a shorter life and poor health and getting old before you need to.....alcohol is a depressant.....it can't give you anything.....why do you think some people cry when they are drunk?.....because it is a depressant.....you will accept yourself as a teetotaller.....you don't want to drink any more.....you can get high with your friends without alcohol.....you can get high on the atmosphere and ambience.....accepting you don't need it any more and you feel wonderful.....and when someone offers you an alcoholic drink you can say "no thanks".....and you feel exhilarated.

'You are now and forever a confirmed teetotaller. Your final decision is made and agreed to and every day that passes reinforces it.....picture in your mind someone offering you a drink.....you always answer "No".....you say that proudly.....every time you refuse an offer of a drink, you feel an invigorating sense of power and pride.....you are proud *of being one of those envied people who has the ability and the drive to see drink as the depressant it is.....and not what you have misguidedly been led to believe.'*

This next script can help you cope with people and things that make you angry in a safe and positive way.

### Anger Release

*'Because you want to live a happy and harmonious life with other people.....and enjoy good health.....physically.....and emotionally.....you have a feeling of peace and tolerance with everyone.....you realize that each personality is a product of heredity and experience.....you know that if you had been born as someone else and had lived through his or her experiences, you would act exactly as he or she does. Therefore, you accept others as they are.....and.....when they do things you disapprove of, the only emotions you feel are sympathy and understanding.....you are in complete control of your emotions at all times.....even under what others believe to be stressful conditions.*

*'This gives you a feeling of great satisfaction.....you feel and express only the good, healthy emotions of love, kindness, sympathy and tolerance to others.....You love other people for their good qualities.....and you forgive them for the acts you disapprove of.....because you know they are doing what you would do in their shoes, with their same body, experience and level of awareness.*

*'From now on you are able to get in touch with your pent-up emotions and deal with them in a constructive manner.....whenever these negative feelings appear you find ways of redirecting them in some acceptable way.....all your hidden personal reasons for the angry, hostile feelings may or may not communicate to your conscious mind..... the awareness that is communicated to your conscious*

mind is  dealt with in a constructive, practical and sensible way.

'Whatever still remains of these feelings that is no longer serving any useful purpose......is dumped by your subconscious mind into the waste bin......confiscated and got rid of safely.....leaving you quite free to get on with your life.....from now on, your mind always starts to process all your guilt feelings......it gradually accepts that because you are only human you have human failings.

'Your subconscious mind finds ways to discard and come to terms with those guilty feelings you have..... no.....control over.....those feelings in the past that nothing can be done about.....you shake them off completely.....and at all levels.....your mind works on ways you can get rid of other guilty feelings by taking some action.....to change what can be changed.

'From now on, you quickly recover your sense of humour and your sense of proportion.....you feel better and more optimistic, with renewed energy.....you dwell on the things you have to be grateful for, happy memories and things to look forward to. From now on, you won't get nearly so upset about remarks or hurtful incidents.....these have less and less effect on you.....you realize that they aren't really intended to upset or hurt you.....they just won't bother you any more.....things just won't be able to get under your skin so much.....inwardly you are much stronger day by day.....much better to withstand hurts and disappointments.....far.....far less vulnerable.....than before.'

## Script for Success in Business and Increasing Productivity

'As you go deeper and deeper, you realize that one of your strongest desires, one of your most powerful motivations, is to succeed in business.....your subconscious develops a strategy for achievement by way of visualization.....visualizing what you want to achieve.....your main goals.....to show your subconscious what, and how, you want to be.....and want to achieve in business.

'Visualize now by using an imaginary TV screen in your mind, approximately three foot across, and project yourself on that screen as a successful businessperson.....do this now.....[Pause for 30 seconds].....this is a special screen and you can change the image with the dials at the bottom of the TV monitor.....you can add extra confidence and pride.....change whatever other emotions you want to.....

'Take a moment to do this.....turn down other dials to decrease negative emotions and doubts.....work on the doubt dial until you are satisfied it is as low as it will go.....work on this picture every day by taking a few moments to focus with your imagination and make the wanted changes to the picture.....now let that picture fade, take a deep breath and relax yourself even more.....

'Each day you find your subconscious guides you with new ideas to increase your productivity....ideas that you find easy to follow because they are in harmony with all your other values, emotions, desires and ambitions.....your subconscious brings forward inspiration and positive ways for you to decide which strategy is best for you.....your mind is clear for decision-making, allowing you to see all the options.....simplifying.....no longer wasting unproductive time by worrying.....once you have made up your mind you can move on, instead of backwards, which is all that worrying does.

'Your self-confidence is increasing and every day you feel even better about your work.....you are very capable of applying your skills so that you work effectively and efficiently.....you are confident in your choice of good financial advisers for your business in order that it expands and profits.....you have worked hard to gain these new skills and so you value yourself and your time is valuable.....your subconscious is programmed now for constructive thinking.....you do this automatically.....you can help your subconscious further by giving precise instructions of the areas in business to be covered.....you notice the areas that you have neglected.....the areas that have caused you not to achieve as much as you know you can.....now these areas are being strengthened by your subconscious.....strengthened and built up with information that you have stored in your inner mind.....information that you have digested but did not realize was stored.....it is there at your disposal.....your subconscious taps into this vast wealth of information so that you can work on any weak links which have caused your earlier failures.....those failures now become your strengths.....when you have business problems, your mind automatically clears, allowing you to see alternatives..... broadening your outlook.....so that you are able to go forward and progress.....and be successful in your business ventures.....problems now become just obstacles to get around or overcome.....and you have the confidence that your subconscious will feed you with all the relevant information.....choosing from your memory files.....which gives you the edge to make accurate and correct decisions that result in your ultimate success and achievement.'

### Creativity Script

'Day by day, you begin to notice that part of your mind.....the part that operates the creative side.....begins to work more efficiently.....you notice this change occurs as you start to take a moment or two each day to re-create your ambitions.....your dreams.....how you want to be.....how you want to appear.....direct this creativity into the area that you wish, whether for business or for pleasure.....the more you use your visualization, the stronger the creative part of your mind becomes.....working quickly and efficiently until it becomes an automatic part of your makeup.....each morning you take a moment to draw a "mind-picture" of how you want to be *and what your goals are.....*

   'As your ambitions start to materialize, you find your mind-picture alters as the goals you see yourself change and your business and personal opportunities increase.....you take time to reassess the situation.....constantly working on your visualization, allowing your creativity to develop..... 'Picture in your mind's eye a three-foot television screen..... project yourself onto the screen and begin to change the image to how you want to be.....how you want to feel.....how you want to project yourself in the future.....creative.....full of good ideas.....confident in company.....a vibrant personality..... imagine the values and emotions and desires you want to achieve [Pause for 30 seconds]

   'Now let that picture fade and project a new, even more futuristic picture of yourself.....being how you want to be, acting as you want to act, and seeing how it feels.....your creativity reaches new heights in whichever area of life you want.....whether it be writing a book.....amazing your work colleagues with your new skills and ideas.....or taking up a new artistic hobby that enables you to enjoy the full flow of your hidden talents.....each day you work on the image, trying out new personalities until you are satisfied.....you can work on your personal, inner-mind television screen to create the changes you would like in your life..... guiding your subconscious to follow your programme and gaining a new creativity that astonishes your friends.....

   'You find your creativity is easily accessible.....when you need creative ideas, you just think the word "ideas" to yourself and this triggers the part of your mind that controls your creativity.....your mind clears and wonderful, new creative thoughts come forward in abundance.....you find you enjoy practising your visualization, which, in turn, activates your creativity.....day by day, you find your thoughts are creative and plentiful, allowing you to achieve your ambitions and goals.'

## SCRIPTS FOR PAIN RELIEF

The first two examples that follow are for headaches, toothaches or pain that occupies a limited area of the body, like a part of an arm, leg or your stomach.

'As you take a specially deep breath, picture the air drifting through your body.....and as you breathe out, allow any remainders of tension from your muscles to flow out of your body.....around the pain, so your body relaxes in spite of the pain.....from now on, with each breath you relax even more.....

'It has been proved that the mind can create its own pain release, so the body can relax.....when people are in shock they feel no pain because the body is naturally anaesthetized.....proving how powerful the mind is.....I want you to focus on the pain you are feeling.....find out where it is most severe.....with your hand, touch the part of your body nearest to the most severe pain.....now place your hand back into a relaxing position.....direct your mind into exploring how large an area the pain covers.....

'Picture the size and shape of this area.....build it into the shape of a ball.....enclose all the pain in this ball.....encircled, so the pain cannot escape.....it is in fact trapped, secured..... take a moment to do this.....[Pause for 30 seconds]

'I would like you to choose a place in your head or body about four inches away from the ball of pain.....now move that ball of pain to this new area.....take total concentration to do this.....now move the ball to another place six inches in a different direction.....take a moment to do this.....[Pause for 20 seconds].....reduce the size of the ball to that of a small pea.....now imagine an area about five inches outside your body in midair, directly in front you, not too far from the pea.....now move the pea outside your body *to occupy the space you have chosen.....picture it levitating, floating.....suddenly the pea becomes very heavy.....it drops onto the floor and rolls on the ground.....watch it roll and see the direction in which it goes.....now where is that pain? It has disappeared with the pea.'*

If you have concentrated hard enough, using your imagination to picture the pain first becoming a shape, then a ball and then a pea, and finally the pea moving outside your body, by the time the pea (which through your imagination has been substituted for the pain) has fallen you have exorcized the pain—therefore it no longer exists. This is a very quick way of getting rid of your own or someone else's headache, toothache or a strong pain that is centred in one area.

For the home therapist—that is, for you to work on someone else who wants to get rid of a headache, etc.—the great advantage of this technique is that you do not even have to use an induction or a relaxation technique beforehand. The power of the imagination is enough. Simply ask the subject to close her eyes and follow the spoken instructions. With this next script you can guide the imagination not only with words but by using finger pressure as a trigger point, which in turn heightens the senses, thereby increasing the effectiveness of the suggestion.

This process takes only a couple of minutes and can be used anywhere and at any time because it does not require quiet surroundings. You could even help a shop assistant or someone you are having coffee with in a busy cafe. As in all methods in hypnosis, it is easier to be guided by someone else. The following instructions are for easing a headache (just adapt the words for other types of pain).

'I can get rid of your headache in less than a couple of minutes. All you need to do is close your eyes. Now place your finger on the part of your head that is nearest to where the pain is.....[Let the person point to the spot, then you touch another part of her head away from her original pain—but not in the centre of her forehead, which comes later].....

'Now move your headache to this area and say "yes" when you have done this.....[keep your finger lightly pressed in position until you hear "yes," then you can proceed to the next step, which is to point to another part of her head].....

'Now move the headache to this area and say "yes" when you have done this.....[repeat the step immediately above, moving your finger to yet another new area].....

'Now as before, move the ache to this spot I am touching.....[Wait until she has completed this, then take your finger away].....

'Now I would like you to imagine the ache filling the centre of a football.....the ache becomes the football.....tell me when you have done this.....[pause until you hear the subject say "yes"].....

'Now reduce the size of the football to that of a small pea and say "yes" when you have done this.....[It is important to give this next instruction clearly and confidently, so that your subject will respond without question].....

'Now I want you to move the pea to a spot six inches in front of your head.....picture it levitating, floating in the air, and tell me when you have done this....[You may find that the subject smiles at this point, when she has realized what you have done].....

'Now I want you to imagine the pea getting heavier and heavier until it suddenly drops out of the air onto the floor and rolls away—now where is the pain?'

It is quite extraordinary how successful this method is, simply by working with the power of imagination. It is important to understand what you want your subject to do and work with her. Stammering, not being sure of what you are doing or sounding unconfident will make the subject lose concentration and lessen your success rate. You can work with this yourself but it is much more effective if you are guided by someone else, although you may prefer to tape and play back the pain-release script below.

This third pain-relief script is for pains or aches that are more permanent, such as those brought on by cancer, arthritis or AIDS. Direct suggestion is ideal for dull pains that occupy a large proportion of the body and this pain-release suggestion is very rewarding either to use on yourself or another.

For yourself, just tape the script and add your own fantasy. To work with others who are in constant pain, this simple technique allows you to help them constructively. Always encourage the person in pain to work with you but make sure she wants to. It is no use presuming she will be an enthusiastic participant, just because she is suffering. This is a very intimate therapy and requires full co-operation on both sides; then the results can be very worth while. Even if your chosen subject is dying, it's the quality of life that is important—and so, help is never too late.

Contrary to general belief, suggestion hypnosis for pain control is actually more effective in relieving organically-based pains than for those that are trauma-based, because the latter may need a more advanced therapy in order to eliminate the trauma. This type of suggestion can be designed by yourself or, if you prefer, you can ask someone for help in coming up with ideas about the fantasy element of the script.

*Important Note: This method should never, ever delay a visit to a doctor or specialist but should be used as an extra treatment to complement other treatments that may be necessary.*

> 'I want you to imagine that you are by a lake.....you are resting and relaxing and listening to the sounds of nature.....birds in the distance singing or chirping every so often.....the trees and grass gently blowing in the breeze causing a slight rustle.....all these sounds comfort and relax you in this special, peaceful place.....notice your breathing becomes regular and deeper as you picture the wonderful scenery.....
>
> 'Imagine in your mind's eye dangling your hand in the lake and, as you do so, the lake is so cold that it numbs your hand.....as you dip your hand in the water you feel the numbness surrounding your hand.....and then.....the numbness travels through your body.....up your arms..... slowly anaesthetizing all the areas in its path.....down your spine, legs and feet.....just like an injection that takes away uncomfortable feelings, leaving you to relax.....now your whole body is comfortable, relaxed and anaesthetized.....you can think more clearly and picture things more easily as you drift into fantasy.....[Continue with your own specially created fantasy or use the 'Steps into Paradise' deepener outlined on pages 65–6].'

Creating your own fantasy can be very rewarding, but make sure you express in words and details precisely what the scenery is like, building a mind-picture as if you were a child and had to write an essay on a trip into a fairy-tale land. Some people prefer to imagine being in a boat travelling with the waves, up and down, perhaps hearing the sound of the water lapping against the sides—other people may be positively horrified by this scene, especially if they suffer from sea sickness. You have a choice of gardens, fields, a place by the sea, lakes, boats, trains—in fact anything in your imagination that soothes you.

## ENCOURAGING THE
## NATURAL HEALING PROCESS

For diseases such as AIDS, cancer etc. you can direct the mind to imagine an army of soldiers travelling around the body fighting the unwanted cells and building stronger, better wanted cells or strengthening the immune system.

If you do not know what the part of the body or function you are treating looks like, just build it into something you can visualize. It does not have to look even remotely like what it represents—e.g. the pea and pain. In order to do some productive work you have to make 'nothing' into 'something', and you can only do this in your imagination. Invent it as you would a play, do a rehearsal in your mind, work with your imagination. For long-standing and constant pain, have regular performances every day. Repetition will persuade the mind to work and encourage it to create a habit. This perseverance will instruct your subconscious to develop a strategy to obtain your goal, which results in pain relief.

## CHARACTER BUILDING

This next script is especially useful for people who find

themselves in a bad relationship which has weakened them.

'Every trauma, problem and obstacle that has happened in the past has been put to use by building up your strength and your character.....to allow you to begin to see your future more clearly.....more positively than ever before.....your emotions now begin to settle down.....all the anger.....the frustration and the hurt you felt before.....and got in the way of your decision-making.....are now back in their correct places.....leaving valuable information.....from experience.....that will enable you to come to better and more constructive conclusions.....the emotions settle down.....no longer on the surface.....no longer in the way of you thinking clearly.

'They have served their purposes and because your mind is now stronger.....clearer.....and more positive than before.....you begin to feel the benefits.....your confidence is stronger and healthier.....you believe in yourself...as a person.....you enjoy your new respect and no longer carry hurt around with you, like a damp bundle of dirty washing.....instead you are proud of yourself and your new attitude.....your attitude is no longer a problem.

'You realize if people say hurtful things it is because it is they who have a problem.....and are frustrated.....with their problem.....you can understand that the remarks and the actions.....that would have hurt you in the past may be a retaliation.....retaliation for a hurt they were experiencing.....it does not prevent you from examining yourself to check if it is your fault.....but this time you are able to do so in a constructive way.....and you are able to work on your faults and weaknesses to enable you to grow and.....be happy.....and contented.

'Your subconscious inner mind works at building and

*strengthening your weaknesses.....the weaknesses that have caused you so much mental anguish.....resulting in a wonderful peace of mind.....as your emotions settle, new, positive emotions now come to the surface.....replacing the old, useless, negative emotions.*

*'Happiness......a sense of humour and a love of life replace anxiety.....hurt.....and anger.....the bad habit of worrying is minimized......it is unproductive and destructive.....because now your mind is open to positive thoughts and you find that you visualize yourself easily and often as happy.....smiling.....ready to enjoy the wonderful experiences your life has to offer. This very action indicates to your subconscious.....your inner mind.....what you wish.....and your subconscious will be instructed by the language of visualization to follow your wishes.....resulting in your happiness.'*

## IMPROVING YOUR LOVE LIFE

This is a suggestion for mending a broken heart and rebuilding the ego after a love affair is over.

*'From now on, your feelings will be less sensitive.....you find you are less vulnerable and less able to be hurt......each day you feel stronger and stronger to cope with life and your feelings.....your sense of humour is restored.....the pain and the hurt you have been feeling is disintegrating, making room for new fresh feelings of strength and courage.....the experience of hurt and rejection now is replaced by positive attitudes and feelings.....these new feelings strengthen your feelings of respect for yourself and your self-worth.....because these negative feelings are being pushed out you find you can concentrate on other aspects of your life.*

*'Day by day, you find it much easier to cope.....you are*

*much stronger for the experience and you find that you begin to see the beauty in life and what it has to offer you.....as you breathe in a wonderful feeling of fresh new feelings.....positive feelings enter your being.....strengthening your new-found respect and confidence.'*

## PROBLEMS OF ADOLESCENCE

When parents constantly call a child an offending word such as 'stupid,' or use words that reduce their children's confidence, it can often create a failure complex. The following script should help to re-establish that confidence. Much of this script can also be used by adults, where appropriate. The script is purposely long. Select the suggestions that apply to your problems—think of this as a sort of mix-and-match script for adolescents. If you are compiling this for someone else, do not presume you know what he or she want. Work with the person so that the script has maximum impact.

*'Take a deep breath in.....filling your lungs with positive air.....and as you breathe out.....all the useless energy that has been attached to negative words.....is released and drifts away.....words like "stupid" [replace "stupid" as necessary with the appropriate offending word] or words that have a similar impact or meaning.....negative words to you.....that are interfering with your progress.....this is no longer so.....as you breathe in, from now on you breathe in positive, good energy.....energy which, instead of filling you with doubt about yourself.....or which just leaves an empty void.....these offending words now trigger energy.....but*

*this time powerful, positive energy that makes you feel great.....the negative words now energize you.....filling those old negative spaces.....that used to harbour destructive, negative words....with positive energy. Let the positive energy re-channel your thoughts.....you find yourself surprised as the energy begins to excite your positive imagination and determination to win.....to be successful.*

*'If you are not happy.....whether you are rich or poor.....you are not successful.....when you are content and happy and bring happiness to those around you.....then.....you are successful.....in order to be successful, you need to appreciate the people close to you.....their hopes and dreams. You may not want what they want for you.....but you can help the people around you to become happy and in harmony with you.....by thoughtfulness.....remembering what they would want you to do.....so they can see you are making an effort.*

*'You find you take pleasure in being more tidy about your room and you enjoy taking care of yourself as you mature in your mind.....taking useful advice and considering all advice before you disregard it.....you enjoy striking a happy medium with your relationships to people close to you..... the new you is encouraged to think of new ways.....new strategies.....to become more acceptable.....why?.....because at the moment your behaviour is only closing down chances of communication.....this only results in making you and the people around you unhappy.*

*'Remember, it is your choice to be unpleasant.....you are in charge of your own life and if you hurt the people around you because they hurt you, you will only end up creating a vicious circle.....if you hurt people by your actions, it is because you have made a conscious decision to. Because you want to change for the better, from now on you can grow up.....act like the adult you are.....and this will encourage people around you to treat you like one.*

'*What you have been doing up until now does not work!.....You have to take the positive decision to change for the better.....if you find your life unpleasant or boring.....you can play a game, an adult game.....and step back and look at yourself.....as if you were a stranger being asked for advice.....what advice would you give to yourself?.....how would you groom yourself for the future?.....your future, that is in your hands.*

'*For the next few moments, take a rest from my voice..... listen to that "friendly" advice in your inner thoughts.....it may surprise you.....it may encourage you.....but it will only help you if you take the time to listen.....[be silent for 60 seconds].*

'*Now hear my voice and listen.....you have looked at yourself critically.....you have noticed what needs up- grading.....changing for the better.....your personality grows and strengthens as you begin to respect yourself.....you find it easier from this moment on to understand what is fair and what is not.....day by day, you enjoy working with yourself.....to improve yourself.....so as to be more acceptable to people around you.....in order that they feel confident about you.....and with you.....you now find you can handle jobs or anything you put your mind to much more easily.....making use of your mind.....allowing it to work for you.....that is the key to your future, to use your mind.*

'*Put your mind to simple things.....taking care that you start to use your common sense.....intelligence is of little use without common sense.....without using your mind to change for the better, you will continue to be immature and life's opportunities will pass you by.....you no longer allow this to happen.*

'*You can only make people happy if you are happy yourself and in this life you need to give a little to get a little.....give a lot to get a lot.....or your own happiness will be short-lived.....so, using your mind, create a plan.....each*

*time someone calls you words which before would have
caused you to doubt yourself.....now these words are a
trigger for your new plan to be put into action.....your
plan for a successful life.....the words which used to sap your
energy now revitalize you.....remind you that life should not
be taken too seriously.....and you can enjoy yourself.'*

And now for a few more scripts to help particularly with the
problems of children and young adults...

## Sample Suggestions

I thought it a good idea to include a few sample suggestions,
written by some of my students, to show how you easy it is
to formulate your own, once you get the idea. Always
bear in mind the 10 golden rules I gave you earlier to
help you tailor the scripts to your own requirements.

### For Eczema Sufferers
*'The reddening of the skin is only the reaction to an
emotional thought or feeling that is not being expressed in
the usual way by being spoken.....it is an odd, but temporary,
way of acting that the subconscious can change when told
how to act instead.....what is required from the subconscious
is, when a feeling or emotion needs to be expressed.....instead
of the trigger switching to make the skin redden, it will instead trigger a sentence of words to the conscious mind that
you can understand and express.....the subconscious will allow
this change to take place as long as you agree to express the
feeling or emotion verbally.....doing this, not only do you
not get eczema.....but your new directness will win you respect
and an increased feeling of assertiveness and confidence.....of
taking charge of your life.'*

### Learning Better

'In this deep, relaxed sleep, you allow your mind to be open.....and information is absorbed with ease.....and is retained perfectly. The more information enters your mind, the easier it becomes to absorb and also to recall....you learn quickly and easily all that is essential to you.....you enjoy learning and look forward to all the advantages that lay ahead for you.....with this newly perfected skill. As the days go by, learning is so easy for you.....and you are thrilled with the knowledge that you need and enjoy absorbing.

'You become relaxed about your learning ability and enjoy feeling comfortable about this wonderful ability you have.....hold that thought of how great it feels to have all this learning ability at your fingertips.....and enjoy that feeling of pride and accomplishment.'

### Stopping Swearing

'You are eloquent and have a wide vocabulary.....so you do not need to swear.....when you get angry or shocked or frustrated, there is no need to say offensive swear words.....just take a moment to express your feelings in a positive way.....contemplate for a moment some words that are not offensive and use those in future.....you do not want to be seen as foul-mouthed by anyone and it does not suit the image that you want to have.....swearing is not instinctive, it is learned from what we hear around us.....you can change easily what you have learned and replace unpleasant swear words with explanations that are inoffensive to yourself and those around you....you no longer want or need to swear.'

### A Happy Pregnancy

'In this deepened special sleep, you become aware of your whole body.....you feel a wonderful sensation of well-being and you are aware that you are the carrier of a *whole new life which is growing inside your body.....you listen to your body and its requirements and you nourish it with a healthy diet and nurture it with thought and care....you are aware that you are responsible for this new life and it is greatly dependent on you, so you care for it well, knowing that looking after and taking care of yourself is also taking care of your baby.*

*'You take gentle exercise when necessary and rest when necessary.....in fact you listen to all the messages your body sends you and obey them accordingly.....as your pregnancy progresses, you feel your baby becoming more active inside you and you enjoy the feeling of being aware of this new life which you have the privilege to take care of.....as time passes, you become confident that you will perform the role of a mother with love and efficiency.....you look forward to the birth of your child and you know that you'll be able to cope with this experience with the help of deep relaxation which you have prepared yourself for.....and with the help of breathing exercises, you will find that your labour will be easier.....and soon you will see your new creation and hold your child in your arms.....and actually see what he or she looks like and how wonderful the time you will be sharing will be. Just take a moment to enjoy these thoughts as you relax even more.'*

## Increasing Your Mathematical Ability

*'Because you want to achieve in your life.....and you want to increase your mathematical skills to attain your main goals.....you allow your subconscious to help you improve your ability to concentrate.....to clear your mind for maximum efficiency.....your mind feels calm and clear as you practise this skill daily.....so as to become proficient at it.....as you work through mathematical problems, you see your life going forward to finer things.....achievements.....you see your goals moving nearer and nearer as*

your life becomes more and more enjoyable.....the mathematical problems become easier to solve.....through practice and proficiency.

'Each day, your concentration and memory improve..... you feel at ease when attempting mathematical problems.....you feel a sense of challenge knowing that you are going to get it right.....in fact, you look forward to tackling difficult mathematical problems.....you feel truly thrilled when you arrive at the correct answer.....knowing that you can be proud of your achievement.

'You're never embarrassed or upset if you don't immediately arrive at the correct answer.....in fact, you will find it easy to go over figures or symbols, seeing clearly where you went wrong.....this ability gives you a sense of pride.....knowing that you can work through any problem.....each day you see a marked improvement in your ability.....those around you also see this improvement.

'In the past, you may have thought you could not do mathematics.....especially when you were faced with a difficult problem.....but now you surprise yourself with your understanding of figures.....and your knowledge is endless.....you now enjoy working through figures because you trust in your ability to learn and remember.....as you use your mathematical skills your mind continues to work logically and methodically.....helping you to understand mathematical processes. You are happy to practise this skill daily, knowing that the more you practise, the better you become.....so as each day goes by you learn to trust in your abilities.....which in turn reinforces a trust in yourself.....this inner trust never leaves you.....day by day it gets stronger and stronger.....and with this new-found strength, your confidence increases.....your self-esteem and determination grow because you know you are achieving your goals.'

## Fidgeting

'Because you want to look and feel good about yourself, you take a deep breath which relaxes you and calms you, so you no longer need to fidget.....these small, restless movements no longer occur because you allow your subconscious mind to help you stop.....fidgeting no longer occurs because your body is now so.....so.....relaxed.....that it is totally unnecessary to make these involuntary movements.....as you walk, your body moves so elegantly because you are so relaxed.....you find how much you enjoy your relaxation.....even in company, you have this new-found relaxation and calm that will not be interrupted by fidgeting.....and you have decided to release the bad.....unwanted..... childish.....habit that is now unnecessary.

'When you stand still or sit, you feel a natural tranquillity which eliminates any need to fidget.....as you walk you move with purpose....and when you stand or sit, you feel a calm and natural stillness which makes you feel good about yourself.....the energy you once used to fidget is now transferred throughout your body.....this makes you feel invigorated and full of energy.....you are able to enjoy this energy to achieve your goals and that in turn gives you a sense of accomplishment.

'Day by day, your fidgeting lessens.....and as each day goes by, fidgeting is totally eliminated and you feel wonderful about yourself.....life becomes so much more enjoyable because you feel happy and confident.'

## Nailbiting

'You feel calm and relaxed and you are growing more and more calm as you breathe in.....this simple action gives you a feeling of deep relaxation and relieves any feelings of annoyance or irritation.....as you become more relaxed, you find that your confidence increases.....you no longer want to lift your hand to your mouth to bite your nails......in fact, you become more aware of this uncomfortable act......it irritates you and disturbs you......it feels silly and immature......and only reminds you of a shy, unconfident child......as you relax even more, you realize that you are now mature and confident and have no need to move your hands to your mouth......it is completely unnecessary.

'If at any time you find your hands moving to your face, you find that your subconscious redirects them so that they relax in a more comfortable position......and as soon as you do this you feel any annoyance or irritation replaced by a feeling of comfort and relaxation......you feel completely in control of your emotions and enjoy your new-found maturity......you feel proud of yourself as, day by day, you realize you no longer have unattractive, bitten, unsightly nails....you now can admire your nails......day by day, they grow strong and healthy and you enjoy shaping them to your desired length......knowing that, whether you are meeting people socially or for business reasons, you look......and feel......well groomed.

'Your fingernails no longer embarrass you......you now can be proud of your nails......take a moment to picture your nails......at the shape......and length......that you desire......taking this moment to use your visualization to instruct your inner mind to allow your wishes to come true [allow 60 seconds of silence].'

## Bedwetting

'Because you want to wake up comfortable and dry, you find you no longer wet your bed......your subconscious mind takes care of your bladder movements when you are asleep......you no longer have the bad habit of urinating in your bed......from now on, your inner mind works while you are asleep by waking you when you need to urinate......you wake up enough to get out of bed and go to the toilet......you return to your bed and immediately fall into a wonderful, *comfortable sleep.....each night you find you can sleep longer and longer before you need to get up and go to the toilet.....any irritations or hurts that you experience won't bother you in the night.....instead you rest, allowing your mind and body to be stronger and stronger, so you can deal with your problems with a clear and confident mind.*

*'This allows you to sleep comfortably and confidently.....whenever you receive a signal that wakes you up in the night, you automatically, immediately go to the toilet and empty your bladder, so you never have to worry about wetting your bed again.....your subconscious now guides you through the night so that you can wake up to fresh clean sheets.....having had a comfortable and restful sleep.'*

This next suggestion is for a phobia that is perhaps more common than many people might imagine...a fear of balloons. This script is especially for children, but the phobia is one that afflicts adults, too.

### Fear of Balloons

*'When children are really nice, special things happen.....when they're really nice and as lovely as you, wonderful things happen.....and one of the best things of all is being invited to a party.....you get invited to parties because everybody loves you.....and everybody wants to play with you.....and there's no secret you love playing.....and you just love to have fun, too.....parties are so exciting because there is always music, food, drink and balloons. But the funniest thing is always the balloons.....balloons come in so many silly shapes.....and so many scrummy colours.....*

*'Some are big and some are small.....but they've only got two jobs to do.....their first job is to look jolly and silly..... their second job is to make you laugh.....yes!.....to laugh..... balloons are at their very happiest when they make you.....*

happy!.....balloons love children and they spend all their time trying to make children laugh.....apart from looking funny, they've got loads of ways of making you laugh.....they bounce in silly ways that make you laugh.....they make a funny sound when you hit them and that makes you laugh.....you can even make them squeak when you rub them with your hands.....and that really makes you laugh.....sometimes a rubbed balloon can even make your hair stand up.....now that really is silly, isn't it?

'The funniest thing of all is when the balloons have had so much fun they just simply explode with laughter.....which in turn makes you laugh out loud in surprise.

'It doesn't hurt balloons to pop and it doesn't hurt anyone when they pop.....but balloons, as funny as they are, can only pop once, so it's best to pop them at the end of the party if you can.....the truth is, though, a balloon popping is always funny.....you can pop one yourself or someone can pop one next to you.....but it always pops a smile onto your face and makes you laugh.....laugh out loud, just as that balloon explodes with laughter.....Aren't balloons funny?'

There are many hurdles that face adolescents and adults in their efforts to enjoy life. These next few scripts can help you to deal with these obstacles and be a happier, more successful you.

### For People Who Are Shy When Talking to the Opposite Sex

'It's always nice to meet new people.....and make new friends.....it adds colour to the rich tapestry of life.....chance encounters often lead to fun and sometimes.....to very special relationships.

'But, of course, it takes two to make a conversation.....and no one can talk to you if you won't talk back.....sometimes *a shy approach is off-putting because it can make the other person feel nervous.....all you really need is your friendly smile and a simple "Hello".....that's it.....you've started.*

'It's a fact that most shy people have some of the best social skills.....but don't realize it.....you may even have thought that you've got nothing to say.....but the truth is.....from now on you won't need any clever chat-up lines or witty repartee.

'People want to meet a real person.....like you.....not an encyclopaedia.....they want to meet your personality.....not rehearsed speeches.....it is important to remember that the most respected social skill.....is the ability to listen.....everyone loves a good listener.....a listener is not trying to prove something.....and that really puts people at ease.....good listeners also tend to be more sensitive to people's moods and needs.....making them very endearing.....you know you've got a lot to offer!

'Nobody likes a bore.....and opinionated people can be very boring.....having no knowledge of a certain subject automatically gives you an open mind....and open-minded people are the easiest of all to talk to.....because they ask questions so as to understand fully.....rather than trying to be contradictory.

'Remember, it is not your intention to be everybody's friend.....it's unrealistic and a waste of your valuable time.....your aim is only to get to know the people that you're really going to get on well with.....naturalness is the key..... you don't need to please anybody and there's absolutely no point in trying to be someone else.....you are great.....just the way you are.....your life will change as you do....and that starts with a smile!'

## Impotence

'Like you, everybody wants to enjoy a healthy sex life.....but sometimes the desire to "enjoy" can get in the way of the enjoyment itself.....impotence is almost always a mental disconnection from the pleasure currently being experienced.....making love is like a roller-coaster ride.....the moment you start to think about your desire for the ride to finish.....is the moment that you cut off from the pleasure that you could be having.....you can even make it no fun at all!

'Making love is about enjoying intimacy, not about ending with a climax.....there is absolutely no need to perform.....nobody is judging you.....and the moment you stop worrying or analysing how you think you're doing.....is when you'll set yourself free.....free to really enjoy the roller-coaster ride.

'The less you rush.....the more time you spend in intimacy.....and the more time you spend in intimacy, the greater the trust between you and your partner.....the greater the trust.....the less you'll feel the need to perform.....at its own pace.....everything will just happen naturally.

'You can only truly show your love for others if they can see that you already love yourself.....this is the key.....you are their equal.....no more.....no less.....the more you love yourself.....the more they will feel your love.

'Keep fit.....enjoying the exercise.....pamper yourself.....take time really to enjoy simple things.....this inner happiness is the source of the passion that you will share and enjoy with your partner.....love is very special.....and so are you.....the longer you take enjoying your love.....the more you release your stress.....the fitter you get and you'll have a longer.....healthier life.....now you are free to savour every moment....and really enjoy your life.....it's not a challenge.....it's a celebration.'

A fear of spiders and other creepy crawlies is one of the most common phobias of all. The London Zoo have had great success experimenting with suggestion hypnosis as a cure for this fear. They have found that an instructive talk on the lives of spiders by experts, followed by hypnotic suggestion, was successful in relieving many people of their phobia. The treatment worked so well, in fact, that many cured phobics were even able to handle tarantulas quite happily!

### Creepy-crawly Phobia

'It's because you want to live your life to the full.....getting the most out of every day.....followed by nights of blissful sleep.....that it is now time for you to take charge of your life.

'It is time to drop the irrational behaviours that no longer serve you.....there is no longer the need to be concerned about insects.....no need for sleepless nights, no need to look silly and helpless.

'Spiders and other crawling insects have all got one thing in common.....they're all cold-blooded and that means, to them, you may seem a positive furnace! Certainly, with spiders we make their "hairs" stand on end in fear.....in truth, they are very frightened of us and, not being aggressive, they run as fast as they can to get away from us.....sometimes when we chase them, they are so scared that they roll themselves into a ball and play dead.....hoping we will move out of their now terrorized life.....if they can avoid you they will.....your world and their world exist side by side, but they want to have nothing to do with you.....just to get on with their lives keeping a clean house.

'We know so little about their world.....and if we did.....we wouldn't fear them.....many insects do really useful jobs for us, like eating woodworm.....always remember that to them.....we may even look like gods.....compared to them we are huge.....immense beings.....to be avoided at all costs.

'There is no need to kill them.....because they cannot harm you.....recognize the "real" situation.....instead of your "unreal" fear.....just let them be.....going about their simple lives.....or if the situation requires it.....put a glass over them.....gently slide some paper under the glass.....taking care not to harm your small, wondering friend.....then you can carry him to a place outside your room.....your lives are separate again, as, indeed, your worlds will always be.

'Remember that fear.....F.E.A.R......stands for FANTASIES ENVISAGED AS REAL.....negative fantasies are the source of all fears...... "being" in reality means that you cannot feel fear.....you can only respond to a situation in an appropriate way.

'You need never react in unnecessary phobic fear again.....from now on you can respond as a conscious being.....responsible.....and completely in charge of the way you live your life.....from now on, you choose your life.....THIS IS FREEDOM.....and it feels great!'

Now let's take a look at tackling two other common phobias—fear of snakes and a fear of open spaces (agoraphobia).

### Fear of Snakes

'Picture a snake in your mind's eye.....I want you to look closely and see the beautiful patterns on the snake's skin.....see how many lovely colours form these patterns and how they run down the whole length of the snake.....see how they run down the whole of its body.....see how it moves.....so gracefully through the grass.....noble and serene.

'Take time to see it clearly.....enjoy these few moments watching this beautiful creature.....take note how very sensitive it is.....see how alert it is.....how it is ready to flee at the slightest movement or sound.....see how it hugs the ground, almost too afraid to be seen.....how timid it is.....say to yourself that you will have only admiration for this elegant, timid, beautiful creature.....that you will never be afraid now that you have come to admire and respect snakes.

'Tell yourself how lucky you are to share moments like this with the snake.....and if you have the pleasure of seeing more snakes.....then you will be able to appreciate their beauty and elegance.....let yourself luxuriate in the feeling of being part of this whole beautiful creation and how privileged you are to be able to share it with such a fascinatingly shy and mysterious creature.

'You have your natural instinct for keeping your distance when necessary.....but you no longer have the fear that gets in the way of that natural instinct.....your inner mind naturally protects you, while allowing you to come to terms with the beauty of life and its inhabitants.'

## Agoraphobia

'You can go outside your house whenever you want to.....when you are outside you are calm, relaxed and in control.....your heartbeat is steady and your breathing is regular.....you are confident and happy outside in the fresh air.....you picture yourself going to visit friends and enjoying their company.....you go to the shops and buy beautiful new clothes to wear.....you receive an invitation and say: "Yes, I am coming." And you wear your new clothes.....you look bright and attractive and interesting.

'Your home is a comfortable place to be, but you accept that you can go outside happily and confidently whenever you desire to do so.....picture in your mind someone asking you if you are staying at home today and you say....."No, I am going out".....you say that proudly and mean it.

'Every time you go outside you feel enthusiastic and are filled with a wonderful sense of pride and self-respect.....you now know that you have the freedom to come and go as you please.'

It is nearly impossible to cure people of snoring through hypnosis, because the causes are varied and are usually rooted in a physical problem of some kind. There is hope, however, for those who have to sleep near someone who snores...

### For People Who Sleep Near People Who Snore

'It is because you love being so alive and wide awake during the day that you also adore the rejuvenation and bliss of tranquil, deep sleep during the night.....in this sleep, your body does marvellous things...it looks after itself and it looks after you.....it just carries on with its many functions, without you even having to be aware of it in any way.

'In this sleep your subconscious reigns.....you travel far in your dreams, seeing your future in the best possible light.....all your plans and aspirations are seeded here.....at night, you love to sleep.....your desire to sleep is so profound that should you ever hear a sound, it will only act as a trigger for you to dream.....the more noises you hear, the better you sleep.....since these will form the gentle pleasant background noises within your wondrous dreams.

'Best of all.....should you have the good fortune to sleep near someone who snores, his or her breathing rhythm immediately causes you to breathe more slowly and deeply.....just like the slow ticking of a grandfather clock.....tick.....tock.....tick.....tock.....the louder the snore, the deeper your sleep.

'The sound of snoring will always bring feelings of safety and calm, followed by a most profound sleep.....with dreams of vibrant health.....wealth and happiness.....and, what's more, you always wake up smiling!'

Here is a script for those who want to improve their snooker form!

## *The Art of Snooker*

'As you relax.....your subconscious mind is open to receive new and important information.....which will improve your techniques and skills when you play snooker.....your subconscious programmes the information so that it is easily accessible and becomes an automatic instinct.....your subconscious instantly stops the bad habits that have impaired your game. This new information will select the technique that works for you, so you can be proud and satisfied with your playing abilities.

'Imagine now that you are in a room.....it is noisy.....you are confident.....the surroundings are familiar, so you are even more relaxed.....and this heightens your concentration.....you focus on only one thing.....you are certain to win.....you are not distracted by the people around you.....they give you strength.....just by being there....they are there to see you win and you pick up their energy.....your subconscious channels that energy into positive energy for you.....to give you that extra clarity to win.

'Imagine now that it is your shot.....you are composed.....ready to create.....you view the line of the shot as you walk to the table.....this is your best moment.....you are in total control and feel coldly unstoppable.....nobody can beat you.....your opponent walks away from the table.....he has failed on his last shot.....you place your feet in a comfortable position to provide the secure base for your body stance.....there before you.....you can see a sequence of shots that register in your subconscious.....you know it is the first shot that is important.....your arm only moves from the elbow down.....your hand holds the butt of the cue lightly.....with knuckles facing out.....everything is now synchronized.....every other part of your body is still.

'You take a deep breath whilst you address the cue ball and exhale slowly as you rhythmically move the cue backward and forward in preparation for the strike.....you are ready *to play the shot.....you are superbly confident.....your decision has been made.....you now execute it.....no other thought is in your mind as you have done this a hundred times successfully in practice.....on the last backswing you pause before driving the cue through the cueball directly along the line to the point of the object ball.....which can only travel successfully into the pocket.....there is no movement in a single part of your body for three seconds after the shot.....you do not look to see where the ball has gone.....you know it is in the pocket.*

*'When you get up from the table you are relaxed and confident.....your cueball is exactly in position for the next shot.....there is a satisfaction in the exceptional standard of your play.....knowing that each day your potential is growing.....your skills are limitless.....your motivation undaunted.....now picture yourself winning.....feel the excitement and adrenalin that surges through you.....you know you are a winner.'*

## FANTASIES FOR DEEP, DEEP RELAXATION

To end this chapter, here is a selection of sample 'mind-fantasies'. These also have been created by students in some of my classes as part of their course study. They are intended to encourage answers from your inner mind to any questions that have been troubling you or causing you problems. The idea is to allow yourself to drift off into a wonderful, relaxing fantasy. The technique is used by hypnotherapists to help subjects get to the root of their problems. It's a form of self-analysis, if you like.

These fantasies are somewhat different to the 'deepener' type of suggestions you have already encountered in

Chapter 3. Deepeners are intended to convey you into a deeper level of hypnosis. The fantasies you will read here have a more specific purpose, in that they contain the key to opening a door which should solve your problem. Your fantasy will lead you to a mythical figure to whom you address your question. The answer will just pop into your mind, emerging from your inner self, and will often amaze you in its accuracy. Try it—it works!

### The Rainbow

'Just imagine yourself on a lovely white cloud resting contentedly.....all around the sky is a wonderful shade of blue.....you are floating on your cloud watching a rainbow form even before the rain has stopped.....the colours are deep and very bright.....this beautiful rainbow forms an arc among the fluffy clouds.....and on the tail of the rainbow you can see a figure sitting there.

'The figure beckons you to join her and, without hesitation, you stand up and step from your cloud onto the rainbow and gently slide down.....down and down you go until you reach the bottom.

'When you come to a halt, you stand up and walk towards the figure.....she is a lovely lady wearing a flowing dress of crystals, each one glittering like the sun bouncing off the raindrops.....she wears a headdress that catches all the colours of the rainbow, making it dance around her head.....it is warm and comforting to watch her as you approach.

'She beckons again and slowly you step closer to her, and she gestures to you to sit down beside her.....she smiles gently and speaks your name.....she says that you can ask her any question that you wish.....she smiles again and awaits serenely for your response.....you know that this is an important happening in your life....that you will always *remember this event.*

'Take a moment and then, when you are ready, ask a question that is very important to you....Now wait until she responds and listen carefully for her answer.

'When she has answered you, she takes your hand and opens it.....she places a token into your palm and bids you farewell.....she rises and moves away and you can now see the token.....you know that this is an immensely important token.....it has a special meaning.....you now realize what it means to you.

'With your mind and thoughts upon the answer she has given you, and with the token now clasped firmly in your hand, you walk away, leaving this wonderful vision of your lady behind.....a warm, comfortable feeling envelops your body.....you now know some very important information that will help you with your current problem.'

## The Sea Urchin

'Imagine that you are sitting on a beautiful island beach of golden sand.....with palm trees behind you and wonderfully, brightly-coloured birds flying back and forth between the trees.....you are relaxing in the warm sunshine.....thinking about a story you have heard about a wise old sailor who lives in a cave somewhere on the island and who knows the answers to life.....you have a very important question you want to ask him and you decide to go and find out whether he exists and look for the cave in which he lives.

'You remember being told that the only way to reach him is by sea in the very special boat lying nearby.....this boat will take you to the cave.....all you have to do is step into the silky cushions and the boat moves down the golden beach and into the sea.

'It rocks you gently as it carries you along and a school of dolphins swim alongside.....the water is so clear and cool.....it is crystal clear, and you can see brightly-coloured fish swimming in and out of the coral as you glide along.....you can hear the sound of the waves breaking gently on the sand and hear the bird song from the nearby shore.

'Along the sea you sail, very relaxed.....so relaxed as you notice the slight gentle rocking of the boat.....you notice some seals sunning themselves on the rocks.....they gaze at you sleepily as you glide by.....in the distance you see a beautiful, soft green glow at the base of a large cliff and you feel very relaxed as the boat drifts gently towards it.

'As you get closer, you see the glow is coming from a cave.....the boat enters the cave.....inside, it is cool and quiet, so peaceful.....the only sound is the gentle movement of the crystal clear water around you.....the boat takes you to a silvery beach at the back of the cave, and there sits the wise old sailor.....he seems to be waiting for you.....notice his kind face and what he is wearing.....you step out of the boat and sit on the soft sand.....and look into the old sailor's wise, gentle eyes.

'Now think.....think of a very important question you would like to ask him that will help you in your life.....have you thought of a question?.....good.....now the old sailor answers you.....the answer will just pop into your head.....have you received your answer?.....that's fine.....and now you know your time with the old sailor is coming to an end.....but just before you leave, he approaches you and gently presses a token into your hand.....you just know that this token will have a very special meaning and is to do with your question.....don't look at it yet.....wait until you are back on your own golden beach.

'The sailor returns to his seated position and you climb back into the boat, which gently glides out of the cave and the misty glow.....past the seals dreamily sunning themselves....past the dolphins who swim alongside the boat.....and past all the colourful fish swimming in the coral.....back to your own beautiful beach where you step out of the boat and relax on the soft sand.

'Now you open your hand and look at the token given to you by the wise old sailor.....what is the token and what does it mean to you?.....now you have the answer to the problem that has been troubling you.'

## Butterflies

'You are sitting in a beautiful meadow.....bees are humming at a safe and comfortable distance.....the rays of the bright summer sun envelop you in a satisfying warmth.....you are sleepy and contented.....you lean back and stretch, and breathe in the pure, sweet air.....as you silently take in the glorious sun, a slight movement nearby draws your attention to a beautiful butterfly that is resting nearby.....the butterfly fans its wings as it sits among the lovely meadow flowers.....the colours of its wings are radiant and the delicate beauty of the creature holds your gaze as you appreciate the wonders of nature.

'You then look around you and realize you are sitting amid a multitude of exquisite butterflies.....their colours are a glorious sight.....the shapes and patterns of all their different markings fascinate and thrill you.....your eye rests on each one in turn and you are delighted and amazed by their presence.

'Then, one by one, the butterflies flutter their wings and begin to rise into the air.....you know that if you want to continue to admire their beauty you, too, must rise up and follow them.....as the last butterfly leaves its resting place, a gorgeous purple flower, you find that you are also rising into the air.....your feet have left the ground and you experience a pleasant floating, fluttery feeling as you follow the fanning wings of the many butterflies.

'You float along without a care as you look down and pass over a beautiful lake....you know you are safe.....as you pass over the lake you can see white swans gliding across the water, leaving tiny ripples that disturb only slightly the tranquillity of the waters.

'There are water lilies of pink and white.....brown furry bulrushes grow up around the water's edge.....an enormous willow tree drips its foliage into the water.....everything is calm and serene and beautiful.....as the lake passes out of view you float over a meadow where cows lazily graze.....all the time you are floating you are aware of the beautiful fanning wings of the butterflies.....you feel the gentle breeze created by the fanning wings.....and on that breeze is carried a thought which enters your mind.....and you know that when you alight you will at last be given an answer..... the butterflies are now fluttering between the trees of a shady, wooded grove....you float on gently.....gliding from side to side around the trees until you see ahead of you a clearing.

'There are many flowers, as here the sun is allowed to shine down.....not hampered by the shadowy trees.....you see that the butterflies are, one by one, fluttering down and that they have formed a closely knit circle of colour.....inside the circle is a much larger butterfly who you know has the power to answer your question.....you float down within the beautiful circle of gently fanning wings and you look at the larger butterfly.....her colour is of azure blue, and as her wings move gently up and down she showers you with peace and love.....you feel secure in her presence and you know it is time to ask your question.....she answers you and you realize your hand is outstretched.....into your hand she presses a gift.....then, she gently flutters her wings and floats away, accompanied by her array of beautiful followers.....you return to your meadow and you look at your gift.....it has a special meaning and may even surprise you.....you feel happy and content in the knowledge that your problem has found its solution.'

*five*

# CLIENT CASE HISTORIES

In this final chapter I hope to show you some examples of
the complicated and sophisticated nature of the mind, and
how what seems a simple problem can be related to an
intricate trauma, so that delving into it can be a bit like
opening Pandora's box. On the other hand, what seems like
an extraordinary, intricate case can often have been created
by a simple thought and therefore be easy to remedy. I offer
the case histories of a few of my clients to show you that
guessing at the cause of a person's problem can be a very
time-wasting exercise.

These cases all needed advanced hypnotherapy techniques
to make the remarkable changes that were achieved. They
are put forward to show you why suggestion hypnosis is
sometimes blocked by a trauma which prevents it working.
It also emphasizes how as simple a problem as, for example,
insomnia may not be simple at all, and why it may not
respond to drugs. It also gives you an indication of why
hypnosis is such a quick method of problem-solving, even
when there are complicated factors surrounding the problem.

With hypnosis, you can find the root of a particular
problem instead of going all round the houses and only
treating the symptoms, getting nowhere or at most bringing
only short-term relief. So many other therapies can only hope

to achieve slight relief for their clients, sometimes only after years of treatment. This is mainly because neither subject nor the therapist/counsellor, or even doctor, has the faintest idea of how the problem began. The specialist theorizes about what may have been the cause and works around that; then, if there is no response, tries another theory. It is all so time-wasting.

Just one session of hypnosis can uncover all the information about why a certain pattern of behaviour began. The conscious (once it has this new information) can then become involved, using its logic to implant the thoughts to change attitude. Then the real therapy can commence, saving months and often years of specialist treatment to get to this point.

In order to find the root of a problem, we have to go into regression. The purpose of regression is to be in a position to recover, through accessing the subconscious, information that has been discarded by the conscious and passed over to the subconscious filing system. With the techniques used in hypnosis it is simple to access the filing system to bring a particular memory forward while the subject is in hypnosis. You can then take the subject to the time, or times, of the trauma(s). Regression is particularly necessary when the subject has been unresponsive to suggestion therapy.

Regression is a natural phenomenon and means that the mind is able to reveal past memories so vividly that it feels as if the traumas are being experienced there and then. It should be very quick and easy for an advanced hypnotherapist to get to the point at which you are tapped into all the information that you need to help the subject solve their problems. Once this information has been obtained, then any highly trained specialist—e.g. a hypnotherapist, psychologist or psychiatrist—can work very quickly.

So now, let's get on with the case histories...

## No Head for Figures

Edward was a shipping accountant with a total lack of concentration. He came to see me when I had just recently started my practice. Contrary to popular belief, which suggests that you need years of experience to develop your skills, with hypnosis your subconscious is being guided by your client's; as long as you know what you are doing, you are going to get results. Your subconscious and that of your client work in unison.

Edward said he had been suffering from such an acute lack of concentration that he was unable to work properly. He was very worried that this was jeopardizing his job. He had been suffering with this problem for six months. It had first occurred around the time his father and mother had died in quick succession. While the death of his father was anticipated, the demise of his mother came like a bolt out of the blue.

He was a small, ordinary, pleasant-looking man. I felt compassion for him because I had suffered myself for six years with a memory loss. The symptoms can be similar, especially the acute confusion and frustration. Edward was in his 50s and so, if he had lost his job, would have found it difficult to find another. With no powers of concentration, he would also have had trouble functioning in any form of work.

The picture that emerged in regression was complicated. His father had died and the family had felt relieved, for he had been a tyrant and had treated their mother abominably all through the marriage. Each member of the family now believed that their mother could live the rest of her years in peace. But after only a few weeks she had contracted a normally relatively harmless infection and died. This came as a total shock to all of the family and Edward, in particular, had not been able to come to terms with this turn of events. There was also the added, suppressed guilt of his feelings of relief at his father's death, causing a tremendous conflict of emotions.

Within the first three sessions, much work was done on the grief and guilt. By the time of his fourth session I noted that there had still been no change in his concentration. In deep hypnosis I asked him if there were any purpose for his lack of concentration. His subconscious indicated that it was his way of mourning and he would have to mourn for one year.

The difficulty was not getting the relevant information but, rather, of finding an alternative that was acceptable to his subconscious. A few ideas were tried but rejected, and then a sort of contract was allowed—a 'mind contract' that allowed Edward to regain his concentration. A mind contract is an agreement made between the subject and his subconscious.

Edward agreed to think for a moment each night before he slept of both his father and his mother. This would replace the lack of concentration forced upon him by his subconscious for the remainder of the period set aside for mourning. This was accepted by his subconscious, which made certain there would be no excuses for failure. Thus the responsibility for thinking of his parents each night was given directly to his subconscious.

The reason why his subconscious was so adamant that the period of mourning had to be one year was that in all probability this period was stipulated by his religious beliefs.

When Edward came back for his fifth session he could not believe the change. His concentration was now as good as ever and he could work without difficulty. He was so awed by the effects of the hypnosis that he asked me if I could put him in hypnosis and make his hand rise to his chin without him physically helping it to do so. He had seen it done on stage and wanted to experience it. I did as he requested and he left a very happy man.

## The Cat(phobic) Woman

This woman's story helps to illustrate the intricate and amazing strategies of the inner mind. I use it regularly in my training courses as an example of how the mind works and how important regression is for reprogramming the mind.

The woman, whom I will call Helen, suffered from a dreadful fear of cats. The fear was so extreme that if there were a cat in the room she would break out in a rash and have panic attacks. She wanted to rid herself of this problem because of a forthcoming change in her circumstances. Her fiancé's mother owned cats and it was important to Helen that she did not antagonize her future mother-in-law.

When Helen was regressed to the first time she felt afraid of a cat, her subconscious took her immediately to when she was a baby dozing in her pram. Suddenly there was a loud crack of thunder which frightened her. The fear made her aware that her heart was beating rapidly, an unpleasant feeling that enhanced her emotions of fear and distress. As this was happening a cat, also frightened, jumped over the pram and skimmed Helen's face. The sound of the thunder and the image and physical sensation of the cat fused together in her mind. In Helen's mind the cat replaced the thunder as the cause of her fear. The fear got worse each time she saw a cat, until she became afraid of the fear itself—a vicious circle.

Once this information was brought forward into the conscious it could be processed logically. Combined with some persuasion directed at the subconscious while still in regression, a change of behaviour resulted, leading to a complete end to Helen's phobia.

## The Nervous Pilot

Sam, a good-looking young man of 24 and a top fighter pilot in his home country's air force, came to me because he had suffered a total breakdown in confidence, to the extent that he found it difficult even to go to the corner shop.

Sam explained that he had been on a mission when his jet fighter suffered engine trouble and he had had to crash-land his plane. To escape he used the ejector seat, which catapulted him to relative safety as the plane was destroyed. He had been hospitalized and, when his physical injuries had healed, he had come to Britain to visit relatives and also to convalesce. His native country was now at war and he was supposed to return to fight again, but he had lost all self-confidence.

In regression, I discovered that fear and lack of confidence had been significant emotions for Sam on one occasion when he was 16. He had been trying to discuss his exam results—the best in his year—with his father, but his father just ignored him, seemingly disinterested. He loved his father very much and this event was quite traumatic for him. I also regressed him to another incident, which had taken place after the crash. On this occasion he had had to give evidence at an inquiry as to why it had been necessary for him to eject from the plane. It was the first time the ejection seats had ever been used and the cost of the destruction of the plane had been astronomical.

Sam remembered one of the inquiry committee pointing at him, as if he were blaming him. This action acted as a trigger to another childhood experience when he had also been wrongfully accused. Even though he was cleared from any responsibility for the crash and the damage it had done, a programme had been established and he was left with no confidence in himself whatsoever. After the childhood incidents had been dealt with in therapy, more work was done on his inner self in hypnosis and his confidence was restored. He was able to return to his country and his military duties.

## Woman on the Verge of a Nervous Breakdown

A very attractive young woman, whom I shall call Hannah, came to my consulting rooms in a terrible state. She worked as an advertising consultant but had lost all interest in her job.

She felt she was on the verge of a nervous breakdown.

She was going out with a married man who treated her quite badly. He was not violent, but he hurt her in small ways that were important to her. Every holiday he spent with his wife, so Hannah was left alone at important times like Christmas. He had no intention of leaving his wife and there were none of those gifts or little niceties which an 'other woman' usually receives. Hannah described him as not very attractive and short. All in all, in fact, it was difficult to understand why she had started going out with him in the first place!

From the brief history she gave me, it seemed she was always going out with married men and generally getting the worst deal out of the relationship. She told me her father had sexually abused her, an uncle had raped her and her mother had tried to force her into an arranged marriage to someone she had never met. She had escaped by running away with their lodger, who was married.

There were a lot more terrible experiences in her life and, on the face of it, so many trauma possibilities that it was quite difficult to know where to start. In this sort of case you can only rely on your instincts and the magic of hypnosis.

There are two main advantages to the advanced methods of accessing the subconscious. As I have explained earlier, the subconscious holds the key to the memory files. Also, it is an automatic part of the mind and so, if you ask a question you get a truthful answer. The subconscious does not have the logic which is required for lying. This cuts down drastically on the amount of time needed for therapy.

I regressed Hannah to a few different incidents in her life, none of which seemed relevant. Eventually I asked her to go to the first time she felt she was not worthy. She went back to a time when she was about four years old. She remembered she had an obsession for grapes—in fact, she ate them constantly.

In her memory in regression, she was asking her mother for money to buy more grapes. Her mother refused and she was heartbroken. Her father and her grandmother always bought her grapes, and so she thought her mother did not love her. She felt unloved and unworthy. Now, viewing the experience in hypnosis, she could 'see' that her mother did not give her the money because she had no money to give. I subsequently took Hannah back to experiences that proved her mother had loved her and indeed still did.

After more deep therapy, Hannah realized she had been allowing herself to be used throughout her life, simply because she felt unloved and therefore unworthy of any respect or kindness. Her self-respect was clearly suffering and had to be built up.

After only three sessions Hannah was a changed person. She ditched her married lover, unable now even to understand why she had allowed the affair to begin at all. When I spoke to her about a year later, she was independent and contentedly getting on with her life. All the sexual harassment and the horrors of her early life did not have to be worked on—she had dealt with them on her own, quite naturally. Her relationship with her mother had also improved since the therapy.

## The Sleepless Man

This client, whom I will call John, was recommended to me by a doctor. John was a computer expert who had not been able to sleep properly for the past five years. Sometimes the results of his insomnia were so severe that his position at his firm was seriously jeopardized.

When John was regressed to the first time he had thought of changing his sleeping behaviour, he was in the office of his boss. It was a traumatic period and he was under extreme pressure. His superior said: 'There is no time left before the conference to complete the preparations. We've run out of time.' So John's subconscious had solved the problem. It had given him extra time to complete the work—time in which he would normally have been sleeping.

I delved deeper to find if this were the only time that this 'time-making' idea had occurred to his subconscious, and found there had been another occasion. As a student John had regularly not put enough time aside for study, causing last-minute anxiety about the outcome of his exams. To increase his study time, he would stay up all night and was therefore able to pass the exams. To his subconscious this was a successful mission; later, similar circumstances established a pattern.

John's subconscious needed to be persuaded that this wakefulness was now inappropriate and was not producing the intended result. The behaviour was successfully changed and a comfortable sleeping pattern was established after four sessions.

John then asked me to teach him speed reading (a one-session therapy) through hypnosis. As a result he was able to increase his productivity considerably.

## *Too Anxious to Rest*

Because of my success with John, the same doctor sent me more patients with insomnia. One particular subject, called Peter, stands out in my mind. Peter had not had a good night's sleep in a year. He was also a very anxious person. He had left his wife for another woman and he worried about whether he had done the right thing. He was anxious about his new girlfriend leaving him. He dreaded ending up by himself.

Peter was very sceptical of hypnosis but because I came highly recommended by his doctor he thought he would give it a go. Even so, he saw this means of treatment as a last resort. I regressed him to the first time he had had problems with his sleep. He went straight to a darkened room when he was nine years old. He felt alone. It was a very empty feeling and he could not sleep. That was it! It was that simple—as soon as he had faced another situation that connected with his fear of being alone, he reacted as the nine-year-old boy. He could not sleep.

I was able, through regression, to treat the nine-year-old's loneliness, which in turn resulted in Peter being able to sleep normally, no longer afraid of being alone. It took only two sessions.

Suggestion hypnosis alone probably would have been enough to cure Peter, but as he himself wanted to know its deeper cause I bypassed suggestion hypnosis and used more advanced hypnosis techniques, including regression, to achieve the same ends.

## The 'Jab-phobic'

One of my early clients was a famous photographer whom I will call Paul. Unfortunately for him he was afraid of injections and therefore dreaded the travel that was an important part of his work. His phobia was so great that he would be ill for two weeks before he had to have an injection, literally worrying himself sick. Paul said he could not imagine where this fear had come from; he knew only that he had been afraid of them for as long as he could remember. He had heard that a foetus can be affected by a trauma to its mother, and he wondered out loud to me whether his mother might have had an injection when she was pregnant with him that could be at the root of his own extreme fear. The true explanation, when we found it, was of course much simpler.

I regressed Paul and asked him to go to an experience when he had not been frightened of injections. He immediately went to a time when he was only about five years old. He could see himself in the corridor at the doctor's surgery. Then his mother took him into the doctor's room. I asked him, 'What is the doctor going to do?' Still in hypnosis, Paul said, without any agitation, that the doctor was going to give him an injection. He was not bothered at all.

I took him through the experience, including how it felt when the needle went in, and he still was not in the least bit afraid. He was more anxious to be finished so he could have the sweets he had been promised. But when it was finished his mother started to make a fuss, which surprised him. She hugged him and asked him if he was all right. She looked frightened and the doctor, too, looked anxious. This shocked him into thinking that he was behaving incorrectly and that perhaps he should have been frightened.

When Paul came out of hypnosis, he was totally amazed. He now realized that there was no need to fear injections. It was just that his mother's distress had got confused with the feeling of the injection itself.

Just for insurance, Paul asked me to give him a suggestion for anaesthetizing himself before his next injection. I did this and he was later very happy to report that he no longer feared injections. He still did not like them much, but the terror was gone.

## A Bad Case of Snake-fright

Julian was 21 and so afraid of snakes that he told me he would sometimes pass out just seeing a picture of a snake in a magazine. I asked him how many times he had seen live snakes. He said about five times, the first time during a visit to the zoo when he was 11 years old. He had been so terrified he had froze.

When I regressed him to the first time he had seen a snake, however, it turned out to be when he was only about 15 months old. He was wearing only a nappy and crawling about on the grass in his parents' back garden. In hypnosis, Julian kept looking at his hand, turning it around in curiosity and saying in a baby voice that his hands were dirty with the soil. Then he suddenly became aware of a snake. His mother ran over screaming, grabbed him and hugged him. Just before she picked him up, as she screamed, he froze with fright. Whether this was because of his mother's fear or his own we did not establish.

When he came out of hypnosis, Julian was fascinated by

this memory, which had been quite clear. Then he suddenly said: 'I know why I was scared.' He explained that when he was a baby and saw the snake, it had seemed huge to him although of course it was only a small garden snake. When he had then gone to the zoo many years later, the python he saw was massive. His fear had grown with the size of the snake, and continued to grow so that by the time he was an adult it was so big he would literally pass out from it—it was too big for his mind to cope with.

I took him in hypnosis through a rehearsal of seeing a snake and, to his surprise, he was not scared in the least. He was even able to recognize that the snake, while still potentially dangerous, was a beautiful creature of nature.

## The Would-be Speed-reader

Josie described herself as a slow reader. I took her through my one-session reading course but this was not completely successful. I took this as a sign that the suggestion had not been accepted and Josie and I decided to use regression therapy to find if there were some deeper obstacle to her progress. In regression it was discovered that when Josie was a little girl she had been made to read the Bible aloud to her grandmother every evening. She was also expected to be able to answer questions about the scriptures after every reading. If she was unable to answer them, she would be beaten.

When she was asked in regression to go to a time when she had enjoyed reading, she went to an occasion when she had sneaked the 'Famous Five' books out of the library. I asked her how fast she was reading and she replied that she had to read very fast because her time was limited and she was fearful of being caught. She saw herself reading very fast with full concentration and enjoying every minute of it.

After this regression I knew there was only a little work to be done to clear Josie's reading and learning block caused by the harsh and unfair punishment she had suffered when she was so young and had thereafter associated with reading. After only a few more sessions working on this, Josie was able to read at a speed she was proud of, with good retention also.

## Three Weighty Problems

### Overweight

Karen's reason for being 21 stone (294 lb), which was to be uncovered in regression, astounded me. Her case is a very good example of how a trauma, if attached to a normal function such as eating, can cause real havoc.

Karen came to me because she had decided that it was time to lose some weight. While she was deep in hypnosis, however, her subconscious absolutely and vehemently refused to listen to any of my attempts at persuasion. I persisted and the root cause of Karen's weight problem was revealed. Her mother, to whom she had been very close, had been a very big woman. After her death Karen had put on a lot of weight and had never lost it. To her subconscious, this extra weight was a way of keeping her mother around her. Karen also felt (subconsciously) that if she lost weight she would be rejecting and losing her mother's love. Therefore, her subconscious had set a programme to make sure she stayed overweight.

As, of course, Karen was aware of what was going on while in hypnosis, this was a very moving experience for both of us. Together we worked through some of the deep sadness that linked her weight to her mother's death.

Once this reason was uncovered and dealt with I was able to reprogramme Karen's mind with an acceptable alternative. Karen was able to lose weight without fear of losing her mother's love. The change was amazing and she found it easy to keep the weight off because there was now no reason for her to regain it.

## Bulimia

Jane was 23 years old and about two stone (28 lb) overweight. She complained she could not remember ever eating properly—she would just binge and vomit. I asked her what she had eaten at her last meal or snack. She said she had had six slices of bread, and sounded pleased with herself when she added: 'but without butter'. This in itself showed that her eating was linked to some hidden agenda.

Jane explained she had always been Daddy's little girl but that when she was 11 years old her father had left home for another woman. Then he had had a baby with his new girlfriend and she had felt threatened and lost. In regression, I took her to an experience when she had first started to eat for a reason other than survival. She went to when she was about 13 years old. She was walking along with some friends; she had just received the news of her Daddy having a new baby. The thought crossed her mind that she always wanted to remain Daddy's little girl. Her subconscious granted her wish by making sure she kept all her 'puppy fat'. Even while in hypnosis, Jane's face registered surprise as these memories presented themselves.

Some further work was done that changed Jane's attitude totally. She came back for her next session to report that she now ate to enjoy—a new experience for her—and no longer needed to vomit as she was not eating in excess.

## Comfort Food

Wendy, aged 26, came to me and said she knew her weight problem started when her husband left her approximately two years previously. She had now put on over a stone and a half (21 lb) and was, in her own words, 'eating comfort foods constantly'.

When regressed and taken back to the first time she had thought to eat for a reason other than being hungry, she went straight back to when she was six years old. Her mother and father had been arguing fiercely and then her father had walked out. Wendy had been frightened and had hid in the larder. There had been food in the larder and she had eaten a whole cake. She had not enjoyed the cake but nevertheless eating it had comforted her somehow. This incident had been consciously forgotten and she had never had a weight problem until her own marriage break-up.

Once the memory of the little child in the larder was brought forward to her conscious, it was not difficult to persuade Wendy's subconscious to enable her to eat normally. The comfort she had derived from eating was simply rechannelled to some other behaviour that was to her advantage. She lost weight easily and was able to relieve her mind of the unwanted memories of her failed marriage and to look forward to her new life.

## A Spell of Witchcraft

A young man whom I will call Ben came to me in a terrible state. He had been referred to me by a specialist who was very worried about him. Ben looked odd and would sit in a corner hunched up and fall asleep at the most inappropriate times.

Ben explained that his brother-in-law 'dabbled in witchcraft'. Convinced that his brother-in-law had put a spell on him, Ben had started reading witchcraft books to try and understand what was happening to him. Ever since he had started reading about the subject he had become totally introverted and his actions had begun to unnerve people. Reading this depressing material had made Ben's mind ill.

The mind is 'fed' through our senses. If you are already somewhat depressed and you then read a lot of upsetting or depressing material, your mind, made vulnerable by your depression, cannot access the essential, positive and light thoughts it needs to keep a balance. This is precisely what was happening to Ben—his once healthy mind was deteriorating.

I began by talking positively to Ben. I did not judge him or offer an opinion but I dealt with what he believed. Whether true or not, to him it was very real. I put him on a programme to bring positive, healing thoughts into his mind, to strengthen it.

He agreed to stop reading anything negative. This included everything from books to newspapers and posters. He watched only funny or upbeat television programmes and regularly visited places where he could see beauty. He was unable to get out of London but he compensated by visiting art galleries. His mind started to come alive again, at which point I did a 'mind-block' suggestion on negative thoughts. If negative thoughts broke through, they were to be changed to positive or happy ones. To deal with his brother-in-law, Ben adopted the attitude that good was stronger than evil. When his brother-in-law talked about witchcraft, Ben would either change the subject or just turn a deaf ear. When I had first seen him, Ben had been on sick leave for months from his job, his state of mind so bad that he had been unable to function. Now that his mind was healthy and positive he was able go back to work and start living his life again.

# POSTSCRIPT

The aim of this book has been to help you to improve yourself and to point out both the marvellous advantages and the limitations of relaxing the mind in order to do some constructive work with it. Hypnosis is a short-cut to deep relaxation. It is similar to meditation, but where meditation simply slows the brain down into a form of rest and peace (and while this can be very successfully achieved with hypnosis), the greatest accomplishment of hypnosis is its capacity for change.

Self-hypnosis is both fascinating and beneficial and takes only a little time to master. It is *not* magic, however; you need to work at it. Fortunately there is no pain to endure while you learn, as there would be if you wanted to become a good athlete, nor hours of cramming complicated information into your mind. A little patience and perseverance are all that is necessary; if you are unwilling to make the time to do this, then it is your loss.

Each one of we mortals has 24 hours in any one day. Surely a few minutes of this time can be spared by anyone who seeks to improve his or her life and self. It is a matter of priorities.

# USEFUL ADDRESSES

For private clients and hypnosis training courses in London:
Bluestone Clinic Training Centre
20 Harmont House, 20 Harley Street
London W1N 1AL
Tel: 0171 637 1320 FAX: 0171 580 8838

Residential courses in the Isle of Wight:
Vectis Training Centre
Tel: 01983 853490 Fax: 01983 781903

The British Register of Advanced Hypnotherapists
PO Box 318
Wembley
Middlesex HA9 6AE

Valerie Austin organizes hypnotherapy and stress-reduction courses in Langkawi, Kuala Lumpur, Malaysia and islands in Tonga, South Pacific. To find out more about these, contact the Bluestone Clinic (address above) or for the official travel agent, quote 'Austin's Hypnotic Holidays' Tel: 01932 765805 FAX 01932 781903.

# INDEX